Young Children
and the
Eucharist

Young Children and the Eucharist

URBAN T. HOLMES, III

THE SEABURY PRESS • NEW YORK

1982
The Seabury Press
815 Second Avenue
New York, N.Y. 10017

Prepared under the auspices of the Executive Council
of the Episcopal Church.
All quotations from the Holy Scriptures are from *The New English
Bible,* copyright 1961, 1970 by the Delegates of the Oxford
University Press and the Syndics of the Cambridge University Press.

Copyright © 1972 by The Seabury Press, Incorporated
Library of Congress Catalog Card Number: 72-86972
ISBN: 0-8164-2425-X
Design by Carol Basen

Printed in the United States of America

for TERESA, TOM, JANET, AND ALLAN

Contents

Preface to the 1982 Edition

Since its publication in 1972, this small book has found an eager readership among parents, Christian educators, and members of the clergy concerned with clarifying their own ideas about the importance of incorporating small children into the full eucharistic fellowship of the Church.

As stated in the author's Foreword, the historical event that sparked the book's publication was the decision, in 1970, by the General Convention of the Episcopal Church to admit children to communion before confirmation. This practice, radical as it seemed to many at the time, became normative for the Church upon the adoption of a revised Book of Common Prayer in 1979.

Considerable hesitancy still exists, however, about the "proper age" for first communion, and in some parishes —and in the minds of many parents—there is reluctance, even opposition, to the practice·of communicating very small children. The basic message of this book, which strongly urges the practice on both theological and developmental grounds, is therefore as pertinent as it was in 1972.

For this reason, The Seabury Press, early in 1981, requested the author to prepare a revised and updated edition. This he readily agreed to do, since it was evident that certain references to events of the 1970s were no longer needed, the lists of suggested resources had become dated, and the language of the book was beginning to be perceived as "sexist." Written only a few years before public perceptions of the matter began to change, the book confidently and unhesitatingly referred to the human race by the generic term "man" and to the developing child by the generic "he."

Plans for the revised version were dashed by the untimely death of Dean Holmes on August 6, 1981. It soon became apparent, moreover, that simple editing could not accomplish all the purposes intended in a revision by the author.

The text of this edition is therefore (apart from a few corrections) identical with that of 1972, except for the lists of recommended books and other resources which have been updated by the editors.

The publishers offer this edition in the hope that a still larger number of Church members will find its insights helpful, and they extend to Mrs. Holmes their appreciation of her gracious permission to make needed revisions.

—THE SEABURY PRESS
The Day of Pentecost, 1982

CHAPTER *1*

The Way We Learn Christ

What does Jesus have to do with Christian living? It seems like a silly question, yet something very like this was asked me recently while I was teaching a course at a Jesuit university on the Christian person in the contemporary society. I had come to a point in the course where the next logical step was to discuss the role of the historical Jesus as the principal referent of the Church's social ethic, and I had acknowledged that there are some thorny problems involved in this issue. Yet this did not satisfy my students, who while almost entirely reared in the Roman Catholic parochial school system could not see the necessary connection between Christ and Christian action.

I am going to assume that my readers have not been so traumatized by current "pop-theology" that they will fail to assume with me that to be a Christian is in some sense to "relate to" or "to be joined to" the person of Jesus Christ, whatever particular problems we may have in discerning the substance of his history. The fundamental inquiry in the process of Christian growth must always remain: How may I know Christ?

The meaning of "making our communion" within the Holy Eucharist is, of course, subsumed under this question. We partake of the consecrated bread and wine that we might be *one with Christ* and that he might be the ground of our Christian action. In this chapter, therefore, I shall pursue the particular manner in which a child would appear to assimilate the knowledge of Christ.

Man as a Religious Person

The human person is born incurably religious. During the sixties it was popular to question this. There was much talk, stimulated by the prison writings of the German martyr of World War II, Dietrich Bonhoeffer, of a "religionless Christianity." Presumably, Bonhoeffer said that man no longer makes the experience of God his explanation of natural or historical events. In the early 19th century Pope Leo XII condemned smallpox vaccination because it was "evident to all Christians" that this dread disease was the punishment of God and to act against it was to side with the devil. A hundred years later, Pope Pius X condemned a moderate socialist movement in France, the *Lysion,* simply because it advocated social change, and "everybody knows" that God and his social order do not change. Clearly no one in the Western intellectual world today accepts either position.

Bonhoeffer stated what is in fact the case: religion is no longer used as a source of explanation in any kind of scientific sense. We no longer need, as he said, "the God of the gaps" to account for the defeat of the Spanish Armada or the hurricane that devastates our coastal areas. But religion serves a more important function than this. It provides the integration of the human community that is necessary for man's unified vision of life. The word itself, from the Latin *religare*, means "to tie back" or "together." It refers to man's craving to make sense of his life, to find a root meaning, so that whatever he does possesses a unity of purpose and is part of a coherent pattern of action.

A telling illustration of man's need for universal meaning comes from the work of Alex Bavelas at Stanford University. He and his associates set up an experiment that required the subjects to push a series of buttons which, they were told, would sound a buzzer when pushed in the right sequence. The buzzer sounded at random, first infrequently and then at closer and closer intervals. When the subjects thought they had worked out the proper sequence of buttons, they were then shown that the buzzer was not attached to the keyboard at all. For our purposes, the significant result of this experiment was that the subjects, even after they were shown that there was no connection between the buttons and the buzzer, still insisted that there was a meaningful relationship between what they did and the sounding of the buzzer! Here we have a micromodel of the demand for an ultimate meaning that is our way of being-in-the-world.

Man alone possesses religion. Much as we might like to think that our pet dog or cat is moved by religious motivation, religion is in fact related to man's unique ability to understand himself as self—to stand outside of his behavior and to analyze what he is doing and, consequently, what he is. This is what is required if we talk about religion as the search for a coherent pattern, a fitting of everything together, in life. We take a look at our self in terms of our action within the world as we perceive it. We judge that action by a standard of the world which is, in fact, our religion.

Every man has a need to do this, and every man tries according to his "lights" to do it. Indeed, we are born into the world as a biological organism, but are never satisfied to remain merely this. We transcend our biological nature by developing the self, and this process is fundamentally religious. It is the never-ending quest of man, asking himself and his world what it means to be a person, to be "me?" Augustine was describing this pilgrimage when he wrote, "My heart is restless until it rests in you, O Lord!"

The nexus of man's religious nature lies in his moral outrage. It was none other than Karl Marx who wrote that religion springs from the cry of the oppressed; and yet Marx failed to realize that the sense of oppression is not confined to the proletariat, but is universal to man. We all must face the reality of truly undeserved pain and suffering, and ultimately this leads us to love or curse the source of all life, the god upon whom we place the responsibility for life's meaning.

Religion and Christian Revelation

Karl Barth, perhaps the most distinguished theologian of the twentieth century, held that religion is the enemy of Christianity. Bonhoeffer was a student of Barth, and perhaps had this in mind when he advocated a "religionless Christianity." Barth himself was attempting to defend the Christian faith from the attacks of certain nineteenth century philosophers who had argued that belief in God was only man's projection onto a cosmic screen (after the manner of a slide show) of his own very understandable longings for peace, reward, and purpose. Perhaps Barth's influence, which extends far beyond those who consciously adopt his system, has made us feel guilty about relating Christian growth to man's religious sense as I have defined it.

I believe, however, that Barth over-reacted, and that Christianity does rightfully and necessarily build upon man's inborn religious quest. It is true, as he insists, that our faith is revealed. This is to say that what we know of God's ways with man are revealed to us by God's initiative, his indirect disclosure of himself in history, culminating in the coming of the Christ. Christian knowledge is not the result of our cognitive efforts. Jesus is given to us as the will of God for man, not just in what he said (and we have to be very cautious about claiming too much for that), but in what he was and is. Because he is the fulfillment of God's plan for man, this revealed knowledge of Christ is crucial.

But the desire to know Christ is the particular Christian form of the universal religious craving of man. To act as a Christian is to behave in a certain manner because of what Christ did and is, and in order that we might be like him. But this is because Christ is the specific fulfillment for those of us who believe in him, of a longing common to all men. Our openness to revelation, to God speaking to us in history—and particularly in Jesus—is a result of that very human need to find a meaning in life that encompasses its totality.

Revelation has been aptly defined as God's "solicitation" of man into being. Everybody wants to be somebody, and as the popular song has it, "You're nobody till somebody loves you." Revelation is God telling us he loves us so that we might become a somebody like him. It is God showing us who the somebody is that he created us to be. Revelation is God calling us—perhaps something like Francis Thompson's "hound of heaven" —to become what in his mind we already are: and so he becomes transparent to those who have the eyes to see his truth in history.

The apprehension of such revelation is not the result of abstract, conceptual thinking. To my knowledge, no one has ever become a Christian just by reading a text in metaphysics or attending a lecture in conciliar Christology. At the heart of religion there is the experience of revelation, first grasped through a basic awareness that touches our emotions and expresses itself in the kind of analogical language we associate with lovers, football fans, and children (e.g., "Your eyes are limpid pools of blue!" "Next time rip his head off!" "Dear Santa Claus . . . !"). Abstract, conceptual thinking follows, as we attempt to clarify and share the experience.

The "tools" of man's sensitivity to God's presence hidden within the events of his life are principally focused in his imagination. We often think of "imagination" in a pejorative sense. "He is only imagining it [and, therefore, it is not 'real']." "She certainly has a vivid imagination." I would suggest, as does William Lynch, that we distinguish between imagination and fantasy, the latter being what is intended in the illustrations cited. For imagination is a realistic drawing upon our memory of the past in order to "image" valid possibilities for the future. It is basic to human action, which is rooted in a motivation that draws on the past and projects itself into the future (i.e., we act "because of" and "in order to"). Fantasy is the product of a mind incapable of imagining, and therefore is symptomatic of escape into a world completely of our own making, unrelated to our common memory or the possible future. Jacob Burckhardt, the great Renaissance historian, once said, "Religion without imagination becomes magic for the many and rationalism for the few."

The ability to play is an essential ingredient of imagination. When we play we test the possibilities or tentative "images" of our relationship to the world. Like a five-year-old boy, playing at being a father, a doctor, a policeman, or some other adult male role, such activity makes possible a positive approach to growth and the future. We "image" roles in order that in time we may move into those which "fit" our widening horizon of understanding and make them part of ourself. It is part of sanctification (becoming a whole person). To play is to bring out the artist within us, what Marshall McLuhan has called the man of "integral awareness." Like a small child wallowing in finger paint, we disport ourselves until we sense that what we have become seems quite appropriate to what pleases us or is most "fulfilling."

There is always the possibility in what I have just said of appearing to despise reason and to be advocating some kind of crass emotional religion. This is not my intention. Rather, what I am saying is that a constant dialogue goes on within mankind in general (if not every individual) between experience and its accompanying feeling and the cool, reflective judgment upon that experience. You might say, for example, that it is the difference between making love to one's husband or wife and reading about the human sexual response in Masters' and Johnson's book on the subject. This dialogue between experience and reflection is an essential dynamic of man's religious quest—but we begin on the experimental, imaginative, feeling level.

A person, therefore, first learns Christ not as a theological principle (e.g., that he is one person with two natures), but emotionally, as an affective confrontation that stimulates his imagination. This experience is the result of Christ's presence now within the Christian community, primarily the immediate family, and secondarily within the larger Christian community (i.e., the parish, the diocese, etc.). In other words, it is part of his socialization.

It is for this reason that I would argue that the grace of Baptism—by which I mean the effective presence of God—works through the Christian community that is witness to the child's initiation. To speak as did the medieval Church, basing their thought on Augustine of Hippo, of baptism bestowing an "indelible character" (brand) in the soul makes some sense in a frame of thought that conceived of man as essentially a noncorporeal, individual soul, having only a temporary residence in the body and in this worldly society. We now understand man in a holistic sense, in which his body and his community are intrinsically part of himself. We become who we are through our socialization, not from some "zap" out of the blue. This is to say, then, that God works to nurture us in Christ through the family and the larger Christian community. The manner in which we baptize infants needs to dramatize this fact.

The religious possibilities of man are limited, but not bound, by the nature of the community into which he is born and remains a part. The self whose generation is a religious act is, to a large extent, a function of his social life. Still, we are not simply passive recipients of its impressions upon us, and in a pluralistic culture such as our own we have a great variety of options (compared, say, to contemporary Iran). But it is important that we do not erect unrealistic hopes for what may happen in our times, anymore than we would condemn Christians of the past for not having greater vision. For example, it is popular today to denounce Augustine in the fifth century and Thomas Aquinas in the thirteenth for their narrowminded sexual attitudes. In fact, for men of their times they spoke with a degree of freedom not altogether common.

It can be argued, of course, that the Christian Faith is a commitment to a trans-empirical, trans-cultural God, and any implication of *simple* cultural determinism betrays this belief. To say that religion is nothing more than the discovery of the self in the process of socialization, not only denies the effective instrumentality of a transcendent God, but also makes of religion nothing more than the deification of society's ideals. But it is also true that our Christian belief is that God is known symbolically, in terms of concepts or models drawn from the prevailing culture. Christ himself, the ultimate encounter for man with God, is known to us as a first-century Palestinian peasant. The classical theological definitions of the Trinity and the person of Christ are made up of the prevailing Stoic and Neo-Platonic vocabulary of the late Roman Empire. Yet God is not a first-century Palestinian peasant, nor does he speak the Greek or Latin of the fourth century.

Therefore, it must be said that as man's religious quest appropriately draws him toward a reality that far transcends his socio-cultural environment, that which he cannot describe in models drawn from his community can only be pointed to as a "mystery." We can describe the experience of God only to the extent that it "incarnates" itself in our life within our historical community. This is precisely what the great German theologian, Karl Rahner, means when he says man is *Geist im Welt,* "a spirit in the world."

The Religious Growth of the Child

The two preceding sections are really preliminary to what is the central issue of this chapter: how the child comes to know Christ. But as we have seen, two assumptions may be made. First, the human being is born with a predisposition for the religious quest, and can be expected to seek some single meaning for his total life. Second, this quest will be carried out in the context of his social world, first in terms of experience and imagination, the concrete and the here-and-now, and possibly followed by reflection upon its meaning. This is just as true for the Christian as it is for the Australian aborigine or the member of the Marxist state. Our task now is to describe in some detail the process by which the young child so learns Christ.

The newborn child comes into the world bearing a unique genetic inheritance which will always be a part of his behavior and will mark him as an individual. But this biological organism will become a self-conscious person only as it interacts with its environment. In other words, the self is shaped by the learning process that goes on within the experience of the dialogue between the internal field of the body and the external perceived world. Yet that process involves, right from the beginning, a desire to find coherence in the self so perceived. This is to say that an infant does not merely "absorb" the data of his senses, letting the field of his existence impose its categories, or lack of them. Rather, by his *doing*, the child of less than a year is, in a pre-semiotic (the "semiotic function" refers to the use of representational images, such as speech, gesture, etc.) stage, "making sense of" or "structuring" his world.

This is the argument of Jean Piaget, the Swiss psychologist, who, together with his associates and many followers, has pioneered in the study of developmental psychology and the learning process. It is of the utmost importance that we understand the basic premise of what he is saying: that from birth the human person "filters" his sense perceptions and orders them that he might discern some meaning. Needless to say, a very young child does this in a very primal manner, such as sensing relations in space and time. Yet Piaget argues that the development of later cognitive abilities arises out of patterns of learning based upon the physical action of the child prior to age two.

A dimension of this insight that is particularly important for our concern is brought out by Erik Erikson, the eminent American developmental psychologist. Erikson has developed a scheme of human psychosocial maturation that divides man's life span into eight stages or "crises-to-be-resolved." The first is from birth to age one, which Erikson considers one of the two most crucial and in which there needs to be developed a sense of trust toward the world as opposed to mistrust. I consider trust and faith synonomous. Such faith comes about through the character of the action between the parents (particularly the mother) and the child. Erikson has written: "The parental faith which supports the trust emerging in the newborn, has throughout history sought its institutional safeguard in organized religion. Trust born of care is, in fact, the touchstone of the *actuality* of a given religion."

In a sense Erikson is saying that what the child learns during the first year of life influences the kind of religious faith that shall be possible for his life. This is prior to any kind of detached thinking or semiotic function, and is purely on a physiognomic or "body-know-ing" basis. The kind of messages the infant gets when cuddled by his mother or her surrogate, the tone of voice, the reliability of relationships, the health of his own body—all these things make possible his trust in a Lord who cares. In fact Erikson has suggested that when every crisis in the life cycle is resolved, a certain strength or virtue is acquired, and that for this first stage that virtue is *hope*. The ability to hope is, without question, fundamental to man's religious sense and to the Christian aspiration for the Kingdom of God.

When the character of the very young child's field is such that he can discern no reason for trust, then all his experience is grasped in a destructive manner. Spitz, in England, and Harlow, in America, have demon-strated how, in fact, the absence of a warm and con-sistent relationship in the first year of an infant's life can result in emotional disorder, physical disease, and even death. The human organism, deprived of a con-text for the development of a meaningful self, is not capable of "salvation" or maturation into the whole person in any way that we can observe here in this life.

In this way it becomes evident that the learning of Christ, who indeed comes to give us the gift of the whole life, begins at birth within the context of the immediate family. There the Christian meaning, which is the basis for a life of Christian action, begins to be built. The mother is the first crucial figure, and we learn our religion not just "at her knee," but far more im-portant, at her breast (and so much for "bottle feed-ing!"). But as the child grows, the father comes in for an equally prominent role as a teacher of Christ, as do indeed the siblings.

When I speak of a teacher of Christ in this sense, a

certain confusion or even discomfort might arise, because we are speaking of such learning prior to the semiotic function and the possibility of a linguistic interpretation of the meaning of Christ (which is perhaps epitomized in the word-event of German theologians such as Fuchs and Ebeling). Yet, without denying the importance of this, I would call attention to James Gustafson's discussion, *Christ and the Moral Life*, of the action of the Christian in the world as learned from Jesus. He divides this into four categories—posture, disposition, intention, and norm—the first two, I would hold, are learned as early as the first year of life. The *posture* of the Christian is that of confidence (or faith) in the goodness and power of God and of his sustaining concern for the world. The *disposition* of the Christian is most importantly that of hope and freedom. We have seen that hope is acquired in the first year, and freedom follows shortly afterwards.

For as a child advances through his second year, certain physiological developments take place within the central nervous system that make it possible for him to gain control over the motor functions of the body. Students of Freud know this best in terms of toilet training. I would emphasize the ability of the child to walk (and therefore move about freely at will) and, especially, to engage in representational communication. We can now, therefore, speak of the appearance of the semiotic function, which Piaget tells us appears in five forms: deferred imitation (e.g., a child imitating sleep), assimilative play (Piaget calls it "symbolic play," but I would not use the word "symbol" in the way he does), drawing or graphic images, mental images, and speech. The child now thinks in the sense that representation is separated from his action or doing.

The ability to think carries with it the notion of the child entering into dialogue involving control and conflict with his environment—in particular, his parents and peers—and both assimilating and accommodating himself to society and its culture. Religion is, of course, part of our culture, and a person's potential for a religious life is largely shaped by that culture. If all the child can perceive within his environment is a rigid, demanding, restricted world, then the only religious meaning that is available for his representation is something akin to a caricature of that Puritanism that II. L. Mencken defined as "the haunting fear that somewhere, someone is happy."

It is during the period beginning with the second year and moving up to the seventh that a child, while developing new learning skills made possible by the emergence of the semiotic function, also develops a sense of his own autonomy and initiative. Social interaction or primary socialization now rises to a new intensity. It is a time in life in which the person discovers the meaning of freedom, with its excitement and consequent possibilities, its risks and guilt. This is worked out in the child's affirmation of self over against his parents and peers and, as he grows, in his play. Erikson writes, "Play is to the child what thinking, planning, and blueprinting are to the adult, a trial universe, so that past failures can be thought through, expectations tested." It can be seen why the strengths or virtues acquired at this point in life should be those of will (the ability to exercise free choice) and purpose.

The application of these virtues to the classical Christian contrast between man's bondage to sin and guilt and the freedom to seek the mystery of life's oneness in God is evident. At this very young age man begins to shape in an almost irrevocable manner the form of his participation in the classic struggle between Law and Gospel. In the dialogue between himself and society, as represented largely by his parents, the demands of his environment are so presented that either they open to him the need and possibility of a future wholeness ("The law is a kind of tutor to conduct us to Christ." [Gal. 3:24, alternate reading]), or they so bind him that he becomes captured in a web of scrupulosity or he surrenders his humanity to sociopathic behavior. In both instances a person becomes a tragic parody of the person who is made whole in Christ. ("No one was ever justified before God in terms of law." [Gal. 3:10])

A Christian faith, in which revelation is a life-giving power drawing the person to a unity in God, depends on an active intelligence. Piaget says that there is in intelligence the dynamic of accommodation to culture in tension with the assimilation of culture to one's own self. Too much accommodation results in a faith that lies on our lives like a "dead hand," and it must be joined to the child's ability to transcend his culture to perceive God's work through the capacity for imaginative play. If it is not learned at this stage, it never becomes part of our life, and our faith represents only our guilt and fears.

I recall once counseling with a man who was complaining of an utterly joyless marriage. He knew something was wrong, but he did not know quite what. He suspected that perhaps the fact that its sexual dimensions were lacking—coitus was "performed" as a matter of duty once every month or so. I asked him what his religion meant to him, and it was again a matter of loyalty to the traditions of the past and a source of moral stricture. He only felt a modicum of pleasure when he was reading or teaching history—events safely tucked away in the past. As our conversation progressed my counselee told me of a childhood deprived of a father who was "off at war," and in which his mother as early as he could remember refused him the opportunity of getting out, playing in the mud, fighting with his friends, and generally doing the kind of things we expect of little boys. Instead he stayed home and worked at being her "little man, while Daddy is gone." He was the product of a play-less childhood.

I have spoken of the child at this age as "thinking," and have said this means the detachment of representations from action. It does not indicate that a child thinks in a differentiated manner or, as Piaget says, operationally. An operation is the ability to make representational transformations. His classic example of this is the ability of the child to perceive that when two equal volumes of water are poured—one into a narrow, tall beaker, and the other into a wide, shallow beaker—the volume of the two beakers of water remains the same. This begins to happen about age seven. Prior to that a child sees all representations as well as all other subjects (other persons thinking about objects) in reference to himself and not to each other. In other words, before a child can use representations—images, gestures, speech —to determine relationships between objects within his environment, he must de-center his cognitive constructs from himself.

It needs to be added that the cognitive or thinking capacity of an individual is closely related to his imaginative, emotional, social, and moral life. They develop together, and if one is retarded too long, the whole process "goes off the track." (It is possible for one to be

somewhat more developed cognitively than emotionally.) This is a process that goes on primarily in the
home; so when the child reaches school his capacity
to make use of the kind of learning available there is
contingent on what has already taken place. This has
become common knowledge to all of us after years of
such programs as "Head Start." But perhaps its implications for religious learning have not been thought
through. The capacity for relating our world to the God
revealed in Christ depends on what form religious
meaning has taken in our imaginative, emotional, social,
and moral life—as well as cognitive—in the home in the
years preceding our arrival at the concrete operational
stage of learning. I say "in the home," but I include the
home as it relates to the parish church, for this should
be an integral part of home life.

This concrete operational stage is itself a period of
development in which we find a child, now seven or
eight (the exact age varies according to culture) up to
twelve or so, capable of insightful thought that is very
gratifying, and yet still not able to learn through the
use of abstract or propositional signs. This does not
emerge in a developed sense until about age fourteen.
Concrete operations have to do with developing relationships between objects or classes of objects. Formal
operations, as Piaget calls abstract thought, concern a
person's ability to think in terms of hypotheses or possible truths—to think about thinking.

Jerome Bruner, a distinguished Harvard psychologist
well known in the area of teaching theory, has almost
made a maxim of the saying that you can teach a child
of any age any subject. Aside from the obvious dangers
of exaggeration, we must also recall his qualification of
this; namely, you can do this if you put it into his mode

of learning. A person learns, Bruner says, first enactively (by action), then iconically (by imaging), and then symbolically (I would say by signs). Bruner taught eight-year-olds quadratic algebra, first enactively through their experience, and then iconically by diagrams. Quadratic albegra, as most of us learned it in high school (by signs), must wait until the emergence of formal operations.

Religion is the same, except that as Ronald Goldman, an English psychologist specializing in the field of religious education, has discovered, most children come to religion classes "culturally deprived;" so their learning abilities in this area are retarded. This is to say religion is first experienced enactively, and then we may "image" it (e.g., Jesus is like a good shepherd or the Trinity is like a triangle), and finally we may reflect upon the experience and image of God in conceptual form. But the formulation of the concept, which is what we mean by "doing" theology, cannot begin until adolescence at the earliest (after age fourteen or, if retarded, even older).

The obvious point is that as a child moves into the school situation there is much value in shared religious experience (if it is not contrived, but spontaneous), about which he can talk with his teacher and peers as an "object" in relation to other "objects." There is also benefit in working with corporate and individual images that stimulate his own imagination and open new possibilities to him. But the attempt to conceptualize in a mythic or analogous form—the very substance of theology—is futile and even destructive prior to the onset of formal operations.

How many clergy have inflicted on their ten-to-twelve-year-olds in confirmation classes ideas of eucharistic sacrifice, real presence, propitiation and expiation, sacramental principle, etc.? Our compulsion has been to deal with the Eucharist and the act of communion as a union with Christ in conceptual language, because that is how we think we know him. Furthermore, we have thought that this is the only level upon which he can be known and discerned. To quote Paul once again, "For he who eats and drinks eats and drinks judgment on himself if he does not discern the Body" (I. Cor. 11:29). As a matter of fact, the presence of Christ can be and is discerned long before the age of abstract reasoning in the child's action and imagination (as I hope is quite clear now); and yet it cannot be and is not discerned until long after this in the manner we often think it ought to be, that is, conceptually.

The Age of Reason

For a very long time now Episcopalians have thought of confirmation of a person's baptismal vows, first communion, and the free, rational choice of the Christian faith in association with what is known as the "age of reason." Because of its long standing in the Church, I believe that it is important that we reflect upon its meaning as a way of amplifying what I have just said in the last section.

What the age of reason might be is determined in large part by when it is thought to occur. More or less by custom, Episcopalians have related it to about age twelve (although there has been considerable "fudging" downward in the last generation), perhaps on the precedent of Jesus' visit at that age to the Temple, as told in Luke's Gospel. In some minds this legend is associated with the tradition of the Jewish rite of passage, the *bar mitzvah* ("son of the commandment"), despite the fact that we are told that going to the Temple for Passover was an annual custom of Jesus' parents, and the fact that the *bar mitzvah* was generally held on the first sabbath after a son's fourteenth birthday.

The *bar mitzvah* itself does mark for the Jew an entrance into maturity, in which the young man is now allowed to read the Law in the synagogue. This carries with it the conviction that he is now morally responsible. The rite by that name can be traced no earlier than fourteenth-century Germany, but the concept dates back to the first century. For the Jew it is the attainment of an age of reason, and we can almost say that it possesses an insight into what Piaget has scientifically documented. For, as we shall see, by fourteen a person has resolved the second phase of moral development, which would be quite sufficient in the closed, homogeneous Jewish culture of the past. Yet today at fourteen a person *begins* to develop the capacity for formal operational thought, and with it the ability to explore the complexities of ethical decisions demanded by our heterogeneous, open culture. For contemporary man it will be another five, seven, or more years before he can hope to possess the moral sensitivity he needs to function creatively in our society.

The attitude of Roman Catholic canon law to the "when" of the age of reason is far less tenable than the Jewish. It is said to occur around seven, and is described as the ability to make an intellectual evaluation of a particular situation on the basis of a general moral principle of right and wrong. No one who has studied the moral development of a child can do anything but read this judgment with utter incredulity. Historically it comes out of that medieval and modern notion that

children are adults "writ small." Medieval art aptly illustrated the attitude where children are painted simply
as small adults; and, of course, in the seventeenth and
eighteenth centuries we know that children were
dressed like adults.

Post-Vatican II Roman Catholic educators are not
particularly intimidated by canon law, however, and
they have taken the lead in pointing out that there is,
in fact, no such thing as the age of reason. Generally,
this phenomenon is identified with the ability to make
a free moral choice, and as Robert Francoeur has rightly
pointed out, moral development evolves in two dis-
tinguishable phases over a period of years that spans
both the pre-operational and operational phases. We
would do well to learn from him and his associates and
drop any notion of a magic "age of reason" (which
Francoeur calls "completely nonsensical"), from our
thought.

According to Piaget, the moral development of a child
until about age seven is through imitation of his parents.
He is not capable of performing good or bad acts on the
basis of his own judgment. Piaget was not the first to
discover this and neither was Freud, who related this to
the development of the so-called superego, that "dimension" of the human personality that acts as arbitrary
censor over all behavior. Bovet gives the earliest and
most systematic analysis of the development of con-
science. As he points out, the child, out of respect for
his parents, (consisting of both affection and fear) in-
corporates a morality of obedience, which is characterized by *heteronomy* ("the law of others"). It is the
source of a sense of duty and objective responsibility;
but, even when developed as it should be in a loving
environment, it is not sufficient for building a sense of

Christ as compassionate saviour or source of freedom.

It is greatly to be regretted that in recent years there has been a move, in panic before the so-called "permissive society," to make of religious education—such as demanding that primary children be taught the Ten Commandments—a means of identifying the Christian Faith with a heteronomous morality. What we fail to see is that this promotes just that kind of religion which Freud describes as an illusion, and diagnoses (quite rightly, I think) as a failure to resolve in satisfactory manner our relationship with our father as a fallible and yet loved person. The stern "judge in the sky" is, in fact, a projection of the patriarchial tyrant of the Puritan family, and is symptomatic of something less than emotional maturity.

The moral implications of Christian revelation are far better perceived in the second phase of moral development. At this period, during the concrete operational stage, the child can build on the basis of mutual relationships calling for an attitude of responsibility to others, including God himself. This develops slowly, not resolving itself until anywhere from ten to fourteen, depending on the culture. It shows us that morality is the result of—not the prerequisite for—relationships, including the relationship with Christ in the act of Holy Communion. For this reason many Roman Catholic educators are urging that confession be dropped before first communion and, in fact, postponed until the twelfth year or later. The resultant Christian morality is considered autonomous, arising out of the self's awareness of others and the need to follow Jesus in the loving gift of that self.

There is also a third phase of moral development, which can be described as the ability to discern ethical dilemmas and to come to some satisfactory solution—traditionally called casuistry. This requires formal operational thinking and is the task of adolescence.

But further it must be said that not every person develops this ability, just as a few never get to the second phase of moral development. The reason is that formal operations require an ability with language that enables one to think in a flexible and finely drawn manner—a language which the British sociolinguist, Basil Bernstein, calls an "elaborated code." But the elaborated code emerges, according to Bernstein, in persons about age twelve to fourteen who have been brought up in a cultural setting in which it is used; namely, generally in a middle to upper socio-economic class. Further research indicates that perhaps the ability to learn a natural language is epigenetic, that is, it arises at a particular period (from two to fourteen) in the history of the individual. Any language—foreign or a different code within our own—remains an alien speech if learned later.

The point of this is to underline the fact that if we insist upon an age of reason, in the sense that Roman Catholic canon law defines it, as a condition for Christian discipleship, we are in fact excluding a whole class of people who are forever incapable of formal operational thinking from the Kingdom of God. I hope the absurdity of this position becomes clear.

Christian Nurture and Conversion

What I have been discussing in this chapter is a pattern of religious development which can be described as "Christian nurture." The assumption is that growth to spiritual maturity is a continual process over a life time. Whereas the general tendency today within the established Church is to think this way, it is not the tradition within those various "enthusiastic" sects stemming particularly from late seventeenth-century pietism, such as the American revivalist, the neo-Pentecostal movement, and the so-called "Jesus people." It is also not entirely in accord with the experience of a great many Episcopal priests who experienced, after a childhood of religious frustration, a conversion during adolescence or later, of which the aspiration for ordination is a part.

The contrast suggested here is, that according to William James in *The Varieties of Religious Experience,* that between the "once-born" (as in Christian nurture) and "twice-born" man. The "once-born" person, for example, is the "cradle Episcopalian," brought up in a home of church-going parents, who accepts his religious life in terms of its traditional expression and never knows any kind of dramatic break in religious behavior or thought. The "twice-born" might be illustrated by some one like C. S. Lewis, who was brought up an agnostic and experienced a conversion to a belief in God of which he became aware, he tells us, sitting on the top of a double-deck London bus. It is not possible in this brief section to explore the nature of the conversion experienced by the "twice-born" man, but I do want to indicate some ways in which we can see it as much the result of his primary and secondary socialization as that of the "once-born."

Conversion consists of the total emotional investment of an individual in the values and symbols held by a given community. In this definition, "values" are those products of a given structure of meaning that a person chooses to live by. Milton Rokeach, a social psychologist who has devoted himself to the study of values, points out that there are not a great many values in anyone's life, and that they are fundamental to his behavior. Moreover, if our values are confused or conflicted, a real problem arises for us since we will be uncertain and anxious about our actions.

My experience and the hypothesis I would now suggest is that people who experience conversion or a radical change in their life's investments are those whose socialization has produced in them—consciously or unconsciously (as, perhaps, in the case of Paul)—a conflicted set of values: idealism combined with the importance of things, or aestheticism joined to a dull and insensitive family existence, for example. Rokeach has demonstrated that a very effective way to change certain values within a person is to ask him to rank his values, and then to bring him to a point of considerable anxiety by proving the incompatibility of those values. What he is demonstrating is, in effect, a means of conversion like that used by the revivalist preacher or by the "Jesus people."

Since adolescence is that period in which we become most aware of conflicts in values, it is the time when conversion is most common; William James suggested from fourteen to seventeen. (Two generations later we would have to extend adolescence.) As James outlines, there are two types: conversion actively sought, or volitional conversion; and conversion that sneaks up on us, or unconscious conversion. The source I would say is the same: the motivation is essentially emotional, arising out of anxiety and frustration with ambiguity; and the result is an utter abandonment of all that might conflict with the meaning of the new symbols (e.g., Jesus, as found in a superficial reading of the Gospels).

It is important for us to see that such conversion is not the result of a reasoning process but comes out of a compelling emotional need. I once gave a talk on "new thinking about religion" to a high-school audience, and a young man who professed to having "found Christ" fourteen months before took very serious exception to what I said. What he principally rejected was my "intellectual approach" and the uncertainty and ambiguity it suggested about the specifics of the New Testament, classical theology, and the sources of religious experience. He argued that contrary to my lack of faith, he was sure of his knowledge because he could point to the experience of Christ in which it was acquired. His knowledge took the form of an absolute conviction of his own righteousness and of an unbelievably rigid position on the far right of every question we discussed. We have in him an example of a conversion, and yet I am confident we would find upon examination that what he in fact experienced was a dramatic reconciliation of a number of conflicted values derived from his very early years.

I began this chapter with an anecdote stemming from a university class that was puzzled as to what Jesus had to do with them as Christians. If I look back at that incident in the light of what I have said and a semester's conversation with these men and women, I would say that what this incident illustrates is the confusion that the Christian today experiences without clear symbols that beget a compelling meaning for their lives. The fault for this cannot be attributed to our Church schools, for this is not the primary source of such meaning and symbols. The fault cannot be laid simply upon the family, for they lack the kind of support a family has the right to expect from its culture. The culture itself is a reflection of our times, conveying by means of the amazing ingenuity of communication the unrelated and disparate variety of man's thoughts and customs.

In the light of this, Charles Davis, a one-time English Roman Catholic theologian, has said that to be a Christian today one must either live in a "ghetto" or the "desert." By a "ghetto" he means something like the Amish communities, who maintain their own symbols by shutting themselves off from the rest of the world. By a "desert" he means a life devoid of symbols. Perhaps Davis is right, but then perhaps not. If we look again at man, is it not possible that we may find coherent meaning in living symbols that do in fact hold before us in a manner significant for human action the God revealed in Christ? I believe the Holy Communion is such a symbol, when truly understood and to this I now turn.

CHAPTER 2

A Theology of the Holy Communion

In order to think about the meaning of the Holy Communion (and by this term I intend the act of eating and drinking the consecrated bread and wine; not the rite itself, to which I refer as the Eucharist), it would seem helpful to look at the question from a viewpoint different from the customary devotional book or theology manual. There can accrue real benefit in avoiding the stereotyped analogies and still "loaded" terms.

One helpful way of attempting a new approach is offered by sociologist Robert Bellah, who suggested a coming together of sociological and theological insights. He presented his idea in a paper delivered in 1969, but it is just now getting the attention it deserves. Bellah starts out from the point with which I ended the last chapter. He asks the question of why our young people are confused about life's meaning, which is for him (and for me) a rhetorical question. The answer lies in the inadequacy or confusion of the symbols that are the sole means of building within a culture and within the individual a clear meaning upon which to base actions. We live by our symbols, which is why Bellah calls himself a "symbolic realist" and describes religion as a "symbol system."

To explain this is to build a conceptual basis for understanding what the act of the Holy Communion can
mean and why it is something which involves the entire
human subject, not just his mind and its grasp or intended grasp of certain reflections upon that symbol.
Such an explanation would begin most appropriately
with the second half of a symbolic realism, and move
from a discussion of reality to the symbol.

The Nature of Reality

The real is not "out there." Many people have the
notion that the human mind is like a photographic plate.
We are awake, we open our senses to the world, the
world of objects make its impression upon us and so we
become conscious of what is out there—the real world.
Our seven-year-old child wakes up in the middle of the
night, terrified by a face at his second floor window, and
we tell him it is not real. We mean that there is no face
out there, outside the window. He asks, "But is God
real?" and we reply, "Why certainly," meaning that although we cannot see, hear, touch, smell, or taste him,
he is *out there*. Whereas God may be more real to us
than the face, I suspect for the child it is the other way
around, and for neither of us is the *out there* the question at all.

As a matter of fact, since the late eighteenth-century
German philosopher, Immanuel Kant, it has become
more and more apparent that we cannot in truth know
the *out there*. We do not know *what* anything is *out
there* (i.e., the "essence" or "substance" of a thing), or,
indeed, *if* it is *out there*. We only sense in our minds an
appearance or phenomenon that is met in experience.
There is no means for getting "inside" the external

world—we must work through our own minds. We make judgments on the basis of phenomena (including that there is a God beyond us), which come to us only in terms of the framework of our own means of perceiving. So all our knowledge and experience is determined by our process of perception.

Later developments since Kant, such as found in Husserl and his followers, have made much of the point that the "real" always involves the relationship of the knowing subject to the object. Many impassioned arguments which all of us have had as to what is "really true" have failed to take into account the many shapes of the human mind and the fact that not until we share the universal viewpoint of God can we know what is "really true" and what, if anything, is *really out there*.

I suspect that this is a very difficult idea for many people to grasp. We have been too trained to think of the scientist, at least, with his methodology, describing for us the real world. Yet Thomas Kuhn, in *The Structures of Scientific Revolutions,* points out how scientific "reality" changes, as the understanding of the subject with the object does, in truth, change. This seems to violate all common sense, but a little reflection will show us that indeed there are many realities. For the real is the result of the considered judgment of the subject contemplating the nature of the object. (If the reader is interested in pursuing this very complex but vitally important field, I would recommend the writings of either Bernard Lonergan or Michael Polanyi.)

The act of judgment is carried out, of course, within a cultural context. Just how limiting a culture can be and in what ways is debatable. Some have thought that it is only possible to see in the world what your language allows (the Sapir-Whorf hypothesis). Stronger

arguments can be made for saying that our total socialization (not just our language) goes a long way toward
shaping our particular reality. Try to convince the
seven-year-old that faces cannot appear at windows.
For that matter, let the agnostic question the neo-Pentecostal about the reality of the Holy Spirit, or the "Jesus
freak" as to whether Jesus is "for real." What any of us
believes to be real is judged in terms of that collective
representation that is the gift of the socio-cultural entity
into which we are born and reared. The fact that there
are so many conflicting judgments today is the result of
the many socio-cultural structures (the basic meaning
of "pluralism") that make a demand upon us through
electronic communication and occupy the same geo-
graphical space, as well as of our individual modes of
receptivity.

Am I saying that reality is purely relative? Short of
fideism (the claim that I alone am right because I say
so—without the support of any logical reasons), the
only denial of cultural relativism lies in the claim that
God is ultimate Reason, and that the proper use of reason leads towards God. Whereas there are many obsta-
cles to such a use of reason—bias, the specialization of
human consciousness, the partial nature of communication—still man's drive to know is testimony to the existence of a Reality to be known by which all realities
may be measured. Of this Reality we have only a
glimpse. As Paul has written: "Now we see only puzzling reflections in a mirror, but then [when we grow up
in Christ] we shall see face to face. My knowledge now
is partial, then it will be whole." (I Cor. 13:12).

This point I have been discussing can be illustrated
by a reference to the traditional arguments over
whether Christ is really present in the elements of the

Eucharist (i.e., the doctrine of the Real Presence)—a singularly appropriate illustration for the purposes of this book. The battle has been fought most of the time over whether Christ is really present out there, or only "in the heart" of the faithful. The Tridentine or modern Roman Catholic approach, spoken of as Transubstantiation, claimed that as the substance of the bread and wine changed, only the accidents remained and Christ was *really* present. But we know now that to talk of "substance" is to speak of something that we know nothing of. Zwingli, a sixteenth-century Protestant reformer claimed that Christ was really present only in our hearts or memory, which is radical subjectivism and ignores the phenomena of the object. On the basis of our analysis, the whole argument is pointless. Christ is present, but in neither manner. By God's promise he is present within the entire subject and object and their relationship. Christ comes to us in this action, as he said he would, and he is present with us as we respond— *really* present. Many do not perceive this reality, and our argument cannot be validated in the chemistry laboratory or in classical philosophy (i.e., the pre-Kantian argument from cause and effect), but has to be supported in terms of our community, our faith, and our reasoned understanding of the process of knowing.

The Nature of a Symbol

A symbol is a particular form of representation of semiotic function. As such it must be distinguished from a sign. A sign is an arbitrarily agreed upon, univocal indicator. It is digital (as in a computer), rather than analogic. It has the virtue therefore of unequivocal understanding. $2+2=4$. It does not take very much to come to a consensus on that. It is equally true that we would not be driving very long if we did not understand, without question, that a steady red light at an intersection means "Stop." Integers and red lights are signs. Symbols are different.

Piaget argues that symbols arise spontaneously within the culture and, if we agree with Jung, within the individual. They are natural, for a contrived symbol is a contradiction. This is not to say that all symbols are naturally self-explanatory (if, in fact, symbols are meant to explain). I can recall being taken on a tour of a recently redecorated Protestant church, whose pastor had just discovered the liturgical movement, and being shown all their wonderful symbols. What he was doing, in fact, in filling the liturgical space with triangles, swords, candles, eagles, circles, Greek and Latin monograms, doves, hands, flame, books, *ad nauseam,* was bombarding the hapless occupant with signs that, in fact, would require a good-size directory to decode (just like the one he used to encode this ecclesiastical cryptogram).

A symbol is, according to the anthropologist, Victor Turner, *multivocal* and *multivalent.* Those two multisyllabic signs are worth remembering, because they are very important for the whole theme of this chapter and book. "Multivocal" means that symbols do not have any one meaning, but have several meanings, sometimes contradictory. For example, brides often get married in white. But white is not only an indication of purity, it is also the sign of death (shrouds and ghosts are white). White, the absence of color, has strong symbolic value in many cultures. "Multivalent" means that it involves us in several kinds of feeling, sometimes contradictory (we can feel love and fear before a symbol of God at the same time). A symbol has more than an intellectual stimulus. An emotional and esthetic impact, it arrests the will and can truthfully have its physiological effects (the evidence of the ability of the "evil eye" to kill appears to me difficult to gainsay). It would perhaps help if, with Turner, we recognize that -*vocal* (as in multivocal) refers to cognitive and ideological components, and that -*valent* (as in multi-valent) designates motivational components. Symbols have more than one cognitive component, as well as more than one motivational dimension.

Where do symbols come from? Mary Douglas, an English anthropologist and author of *Natural Symbols,* argues that symbols must be understood as arising from out of society. Where there are no clearcut group boundaries and where the status of the self is undifferentiated, there is a confusion as to symbols. She suggests that this is the case today, and the Church's willingness to abrogate many symbols (e.g., the Friday fast) and to embrace a kind of anti-ritualism in favor of ethicalism is a surrender to the "spirit of our times" and a grave disservice to its people. Others have noted this pattern, but insist that since we cannot create out of nothing a symbolic pattern, we have no choice. Meaning is collapsing and with it our values. This would support Charles Davis' statement that a Christian today must live either in the "ghetto" (an isolated socio-cultural structure, living by its own symbols) or the desert (a world without symbols).

Although Mrs. Douglas does not seem as clear as she might be on this subject, and consequently I may not grasp her full intention, it does seem to me that we are never completely devoid of symbols. Life itself carries a certain structure, and there are certain universal symbols that partake of human life itself; in particular, life as conception, birth and incorporation. This is why the meal, sexuality, and the emergence into new life are found in the ritual of almost all religions—if ritual is understood as a collection of symbols. The Church has, we immediately recognize, made central use of birth and incorporation in Baptism and Holy Communion. Although it has understandably avoided some pagan rites involving sexuality, such as temple prostitution (which, while not approving, we might view a little more sympathetically than some puritanical commentators), the Church finds itself with such symbols, particularly in popular devotions centering in the Mother of Jesus.

When the society lacks a clear sense of group identity, such as is the case today in our heterogeneous socio-cultural world, a symbolic reality must take on a more personal cast. The society does not support our symbols, and we have to look to our own life. There is a stripping away of external symbols, which needs to be countered by an encouragement of such symbols as are universal to human experience. This includes an active encouragement of the experience of them as symbolic.

For a symbol is a means of participation in that which we cannot know any other way. We cannot know God apart from the symbolic. Mrs. Douglas illustrates this in a way which quite accords with my conversations with members of the New Left. She says current revolutionary and utopian schemes which are iconoclastic are also lacking in any clear meaning as to what they strive to institute in place of the admittedly impersonal and rigid contemporary system. Symbols do die, but we need to look for others that may take their place as a new socio-cultural entity emerges. This is what is happening now, and this is what we need to be about as we reshape our rituals. But, in the meantime, there are those symbols which are fundamental to human existence, and at such times as these we become particularly dependent upon them.

It would appear to me that the Church needs to concentrate upon recovering the symbolic power latent within baptism, perhaps returning to immersion and even nudity as a means of dramatizing its relation to birth or emergence from the "waters" of the womb, as well as mankind's apparent evolution from the waters of the ocean. It is obvious to any astute observer, no matter what his personal point of view, that in our society human sexuality is an extremely powerful symbol, be it exemplified in the violent protest against sex education or in its effective use in advertising. We need to harness its power as well, which will require our getting behind the juridical nonsense that afflicts our theology of marriage as well as the impoverishment of sexuality by the women's liberation movement, in order to discern what it really means to join with the body of another. If this seems to suggest something almost gross in religion, perhaps an observation by the French Roman Catholic liturgiologist Fr. M. D. Chenu, is helpful; namely, that ritual ought to border on the vulgar if it is to affect our lives. If this appears to contradict the rhetoric of the Society for the Preservation of the Book of Common Prayer and *Christian Challenge*, in their appeal for the retention of "Anglican good taste," I am glad. Their spokesmen may be well intentioned, but they do not understand the nature of liturgy.

The greatest need is to call attention to the meaning carried within the fellowship of the meal. Yet before turning in more detail to this, one brief clarification is called for. Sacraments are symbols. As some have suggested, there is value, however, in using the term "sacrament" to refer only to those symbols in which the Church teaches that God has promised to be present to man for our response. If it helps to embrace the decision of the Fourth Lateran Council (1215) and say there are seven such sacraments, I am all for it. I personally find numerology and the importance of the number "seven" unappealing. Without doubt, Protestant iconoclasm, which attempted to reduce the number, is an example of symbolic impoverishment which comes from a nonreflective surrender to the literalism of the age. Without an exact count, probably there are many more than seven sacraments.

Holy Communion as Symbol

We are what we eat. This familiar axiom is often taken for the cynical observation of the materialist, while in truth it can be the basis of the understanding of the meaning of that most Christian action, the Holy Communion.

No one questions the fact that all organic life, including man, sustains existence by absorbing the chemical elements appropriate to it by means of incorporation and assimilation—taking into ourself needed nutriments and, indeed, becoming one with the elements within that material, while expelling the unabsorbed. In terms of human evolution it becomes interesting to speculate as to what material man chooses to incorporate. It has been argued that before being forced down from the trees of Africa's diminishing forests our ancestors were vegetarians, and only when the scarcity of such food amid the expanding grasslands threatened the anthropoids with starvation were we forced to eat meat and, consequently, changed our pattern or behavior. In this way it can be argued that what we eat has to do with how we behave.

But the incorporative image is more sophisticated and subtle than this. Eating is prototypical, psychologists tell us, of man's most primal orientation to the world. He begins to develop the self in terms of all his senses through the incorporation of the exterior world, and continues to do this through his life. Just as the infant sucks and later bites and chews his food that the food itself might be his, so does he incorporate through all his senses the behavior of others and makes it his own by the slow process of assimilation. This is no more premeditated than digestion itself. While the identification of the self in this manner occupies primarily the early years, such incorporation of the observed world continues to refine our self until death.

The absorption of univocal behavior, such as the significative demands of society (e.g., a gentleman brushes his teeth after every meal), does not present the self with any option but accommodation to society. In this sense, the individual is the product of the social fact. But phenomena confronting us as symbolic call upon us for imaginative response, which enables us to discover within it the possibilities for our life. As Piaget has said, play is a very early form of symbol that takes on importance for the child when he reaches the age of three, four, five and six—the age, above all others, of the imagination (although, we devoutly hope, not the only time for the exercise of the imagination). Indeed, the child of this age is altogether open to the symbol. He cannot, however, *reflect* conceptually upon its possible meaning for him.

If we eat the same thing we become the same. This follows logically from the original thesis that we are what we eat. We become one with the other when we share a meal. The dramatic action that undergirds this in pre-eighteenth-century table manners is obscured for us, for these people ate from the same dish, drank from the common cup, and chewed on the one bone. Yet the emotional impact of the shared meal is not lost to us. In the mid-fifties in the South the bitter humor of the printed cards, passed among resentful whites, reading, "Support integration—take a nigger out to lunch," was rooted in that universal human experience that to eat with someone is not only to acknowledge him as an equal but to become one with him analogous to the union found in sexual intercourse. I well recall that as a boy, growing up in North Carolina, my mother, while a very gracious and moral person, still kept separate eating utensils for our black gardener. With a reaction I recall vividly, she expressed genuine disgust at my one-time inadvertent use of his drinking glass. In one of my first cures my black warden would not think of sitting down to eat with me (although, obviously and interestingly enough, we did eat together at the altar).

We know that in many cultures, past and present, to share a meal with another person acknowledges a relationship to him that forbids aggressive action toward him. Where the group bond is considered more important than our individual identity, such a person, by the act of eating with us, enters within our corporate self. Such a feeling is, perhaps, rooted in our unknown past, growing out of the need for man to hunt in bands and to trust explicitly those with whom he stalked and killed the wild beasts, and then shared the fruits of their common daring. Lionel Tiger, a Canadian ethologist, claims that the "loving cup," the fraternity mug, and particularly the sacred chalice—as symbols of the group bond—all have their roots in the practice of primitive man to drink the blood of his enemies from the skull cap of the unfortunate victim.

As primitive man sought to understand this mysterious feeling of drawing together in the shared meal, it would seem he came to the act of eating the flesh and especially drinking the blood of the other as an acquisition of the life—particularly the strengths or virtues—of the victim. ("But you must not eat the flesh with the life, which is the blood, still in it." [Gen. 9:4] "Unless you eat the flesh of the Son of Man and drink his blood you can have no life in you." [Jn. 6:53]) Cannibalism could be rationalized in this manner. We honor a brave enemy by eating him, that we might acquire his bravery; just as we eat the flesh of the deer that we might become as swift as he. As life was identified with the body and, particularly, the blood, so the meal came to take on a sacred quality as it became a mysterious means of contact with the source of all life and, consequently, of all meaning.

A more spiritualized form of the same theme, was the ancient Roman custom for families to go to the cemetery on certain dates after the death of a member and to share a meal there with his soul, which they believed inhabited the area of his tomb. In this way it was believed the gulf between the living and the dead was crossed and the unity of the family maintained. It is interesting to speculate concerning the impact of such practices upon the development of the Christian custom of the requiem Eucharist and the cult of the saints.

The sacred meal was and is very much a part of the Jewish cultus. Perhaps we shall never solve the question of just what kind of meal it was at which Jesus is described as instituting the Sacrament of his Body and Blood, but the obvious fact is that union with him is set in the context of the symbol so universal to man, the sharing of food and drink within a community. The impact of that simple commemoration remains still great today because it is rooted in man's fundamental experience of his own history.

It would appear that the sacrificial cultus, lost to Jewish faith after A.D. 70, but common to pagan religions, is intimately related to the sacred meal. When man offered to God an animal victim and ate part of the oblation, or when he poured on the ground a bit of the wine as a libation, the action was of a meal that is shared with God. In some equivocal sense, by directing this common yet mysterious human experience of communal eating to the divine, man experienced a oneness with the source of life. Within his imagination (and that is a positive word) he sensed the coherence for which all men strive. It was not so much his "theology," the conceptual ordering of reflection upon the experience, but the multivalent involvement of the total man —emotions, will, body and mind—in the symbol that drew him on. It is not for us to despise this expression which is only another way of grasping that same elusive truth we seek when we draw around the family table at Thanksgiving.

This being part of our religious history, it is altogether understandable that the early Church, reflecting upon the Christian meal, related it to Christ's sacrifice on Calvary. Again Paul provides us with the insight. "For every time you eat this bread and drink this cup, you proclaim the death of the Lord, until he comes." (I Cor. 11:26) It is by his death that life and meaning become a possibility for man, and this life becomes ours in the symbol of the bread and wine, his Body and Blood, which we eat and drink. The Romans called the early Christians "cannibals." While the charge was in one sense scurrilous and repulsive, in another way it touched upon a deep and universal symbol within man's consciousness and is profoundly true.

The Holy Communion is then a symbolic act in which the mystery of God-coming-to-man in Christ and his death engages the imagination and consequently the total person that participates. What is at stake is life and meaning, unity and coherence.

Revelation and Mystery

It would appear that in the last section I have spoken much more of religion and man's ways of seeking God than I have of revelation and God's ways of soliciting man. It would be a gross error in any discussion of the Holy Communion and its meaning as symbol to pass without some further elaboration of the meaning of the revelational dimension of the symbol.

The inner life of the Godhead is not knowable to man. The finite cannot begin to comprehend the infinite, and ultimately *God is mystery*. He lies beyond man's limits, and man only knows the limits. Paradoxically, we might say that the source of all light for man is in utter darkness. It is like a shaft of light we are unaware of until it hits an object, and then we still have no direct knowledge. Similarly, what man knows of this mystery he knows only symbolically; that is to say, in terms of his finite, material existence. It is always God acting in and through the symbols. If this were not so, the only alternate would be man's projection of his own wishes into the so-called symbols. The perception of God's action is, therefore, man's imagination *charged or empowered by faith*. There is no rational proof that God is "there."

Perhaps this is something which in our efforts to reform the Church's liturgy we miss. Is it not possible that in trying to capture the exact meaning of the experience of God in clear English we create a lessening of the likelihood of that same experience? In the ambiguity and murky meaning of sixteenth-century English there is a sense of encounter with the numinous. It is the same phenomenon as in poetry. Some of us will complain of the greatest poets that their meaning is obscure. But perhaps this is exactly what is intended. The pattern of sound and the combination of words, unobstructed by explicit definition, will perhaps evoke a meaning that is not of our making but that comes to us out of the "mystery."

Victor Turner, in his analysis as an anthropologist of the nature of symbols, points out that the most powerful symbols emerge from the *penumbra,* the "cosmic shadows" that surround our life, into which no light of human logic can pierce and upon which we can only wait for illumination. He speaks of the *liminal* ("threshold") experience as fundamental to the nature of this illumination. Another way of phrasing this concept is to suggest that mystery best evokes a new awareness by means of the incongruous, that which does not "fit" our socio-culturally conditioned categories. Humor and fear are two emotions evoked by such incongruity, and they lie very close to the experience of the numinous. At the same time, they stimulate man's imagination as well as his fantasies.

Dorothy Sayers has described Christ's power as the

attraction of incongruity: man and God manifested in one person. We are so used to the words we lose their absurdity and therefore the possible meaning of the symbol. For Christ is the ultimate symbol. The Dutch theologian, Schillebeeckx, has described this as the "sacrament of encounter with God." He is the supreme symbol of the mystery. "That life was the light of men. The light shines on in the dark, and the darkness has never mastered it . . . . he came to dwell among us, and we saw his glory." (Jn. 1:4-5, 14). "Glory" means the veiled manifestation of the mystery that is the God-no-man-ever-sees. The historical Jesus was he whom the light struck out of the penumbra from beyond the limitations of our reason, from where we can exercise no control, but can only wait. He was that light, as well, and hence the incongruity, the power of the symbol.

Words can be symbols, but only those words that draw us beyond their assigned meaning to images that emerge from what cannot be articulated. Not every word can do this, and least of all the sterile propositions of man's philosophic gropings. Persons and their actions have more power. Jesus came not so much to say—we know really very little of what he actually said and most of the reported sayings lack originality—but to be and to do. This was the heart of his symbolic power. It was in this that he most clearly pointed to the mystery from which he came and to which he returned. It is for this reason that while Karl Rahner has said that there are three mysteries in Christian faith—the Trinity, the nature of God's action in Creation; the Incarnation, the focus of that action in the coming of Christ; and Grace, the continued presence of God, shaping in his image the lives of men—there is really only one: Jesus. For in his action all three are revealed.

Yet we speak of the Holy Eucharist as the Holy Mysteries. The term is applicable only, and yet in a most important way, by association. The symbol of Holy Communion evokes our participation in the action of Christ and opens to us the meaning of his life. In him, perceived in this way, the mystery of God reveals him to us and, through our participation, draws us to himself. The eucharist life is always a life played out on the edge of that mystery from which Christ came and to which he has gone. It is not for those who want things simple, straightforward, and neat.

The Proper Participant in the Symbol of Holy Communion

It could be said that everything to this point has been by way of introduction, or that this section is the *apogee* of the discussion. For inasmuch as the motivation of this study is the revisions in the long-standing practice of the Episcopal Church as to who shall be admitted to communion, all that has gone before is clearly an exposition of the logic of that change. I have not tried to veil my sympathies, but the data is there to see as well.

Pope Pius X directed in 1910 that a child should be admitted to communion when he knew the difference between the Eucharist as a sacred meal and the family meal. This was generally interpreted as about age seven. The basis for this practice is a separation that Italian theology persistently makes, which seems very questionable: an implicit dualism between nature and supernature. On the contrary, I would argue that every meal is open to sacrality, and the family meal naturally draws us to the sacred meal of the Eucharist.

Prayer Book Study 18 suggested that the child should

never be unable to remember making his communion, on the theory that it is, in fact, a "natural" thing for him to do—just as natural as coming to the family table, once he is physically capable of sitting and feeding himself and being a not-altogether-unpleasant presence there. This would seem to place admission to Holy Communion at the beginning of the pre-operational cognitive period, where the semiotic function (necessary for memory) begins to emerge, rather than at the end of that period. This would be at age three or four.

I would have to say, however, that in all fairness a case can be made for communion at even an earlier age, even before a child is weaned and long before the emergence of the semiotic function. On the subject of children and communion, I have spoken with a number of clergy who feel very strongly about this, and good support can be found for their position in a paper by Erik Erikson, "The Development of Ritualization." There Erikson argues that in the mutuality of recognition that takes place between the infant and the mother there is more than mere supplying of practical wants; there is a fulfillment of emotional and spiritual needs; there is the experience of separateness transcended and distinctiveness confirmed—"a sense of being lifted up to the very bosom of the supernatural." In this ritual confirmation of the infant's religious quest, related to his life with his mother, there is found the numinous, the "hallowed presence" of the other, upon which some would insist we need to build the act of communion in the Holy Eucharist.

The actual decision about the age a child shall make his communion has been left up to local—diocesan or parochial—leadership, and the practice varies widely. Some are ignoring this option and it is "business as usual." Others are communicating infants in arms, and a great many are simply picking an age in between. Certainly, what age we choose determines what preparation is appropriate (as we shall see in the next two chapters). My brief here is that what we did up until 1970, and the arguments we have used to support it, do not accord with the data—psychological, anthropological, sociological, and theological—and that it is much easier to say we need to change to an earlier age than it is to say precisely to what age. Speaking for myself, I am inclined to think that Pope Pius waits too long, but that if we do anything before the emergence of the play function (age three or so) we had better be sure that we are not just kidding ourselves about its effect.

I suspect that the reader can elicit, from what has been said so far, my reasons for this conclusion. In the way of clarification and summation, we can discern at least five reasons for the wisdom of admitting young children to communion after baptism, but before confirmation. Having stated these, less I be misunderstood, I will conclude with a section providing one very important *caveat*.

First, there is the negative reason. The ability to reflect, to make judgments, to engage in formal operations is not necessary for the beneficial experience of a symbol. A symbol engages us on more levels of motivation than our reason (it is multivalent), and it would be simply wrong to think that someone who made his communion without a conceptual grasp of its meaning could not derive anything but harm from the act. As a matter of fact, I am extremely doubtful as to the benefit of maintaining a conceptual approach at the moment of participating in any symbol. It makes a univocal sign out of a multivocal symbol.

Some would want to argue, perhaps, that Anglicanism has always placed high value on reason and that this violates our tradition. As we shall see, there is cause to be proud of our rational tradition, and this whole study is an exercise in that spirit. The argument is beside the point however. Furthermore, it is important to avoid that sterility of spirit that beset Christianity during the seventeenth century, often characterized as the period of "classical Anglicanism," which can be typified as preferring a ten-minute analysis on the Lord's Prayer *in lieu* of saying the Lord's Prayer! It was this devotion to rationality for its own sake that begot the sentimentality and anti-rationality of pietism; and it is what is now provoking a neo-Pietism, with all its attendant misconceptions, in neo-Pentecostalism and the so-called "Jesus movement."

Gabriel Moran, a leading Roman Catholic catechetical theologian, has made the point repeatedly that theology is for adults, but has equally emphasized that religion is for everyone. The act of making our communion is a religious act *per se*, possessing important theological implications not essential to its efficacy!

Second, there is the theological reason. There are no "associate" or "junior" members of the Church. Baptism admits one to full membership in the Body of Christ, as the Prayer Book Catechism states. I would not want to dismiss lightly the value of what we know as Confirmation, although efforts to vindicate its necessary role in Christian initiation theologically have failed and the pastoral use of the rite is notoriously inept. Historically, its existence has all the signs of an "accident."

Yet Anglicans—and generally only Anglicans—have made a postponed rite of Confirmation a prerequisite to

Holy Communion. Why? As with many things, we have made a theory out of an expedience. Archbishop Peckham of Canterbury (1279-1292) was introduced to that see by Pope Nicholas III for the purpose of instituting many papal reforms. One of the results was a decree from Lambeth in 1281 in which he sought to stop negligence concerning Confirmation, and so ordered that no one could make their communion until after they were confirmed. It might be added that at the time frequent communion under any circumstances was generally unknown. The implications of this decree reached absurd proportions in a tradition epitomized by William Augustus Muhlenberg, an eminent nineteenth-century American churchman, who suggested that Confirmation and Holy Communion be separated by two years, as he believed we ought to take "one step at a time."

We find ourselves today in possession of a body of rationalizations upon unexamined practices, which are the result of historical happenstance no longer applicable. The need is to begin with our theology and not our history, and this is what we have done in the actions of recent General Conventions. This is not to say that the pressure of the times influences us any less than the Church in the fourth or thirteenth centuries.

Third, there is the psychological reason. Many children at an early age—say age three or so—are quite capable and particularly receptive to the symbolic experience. Symbolism requires that imagination and openness to life allow us to play with new ideas and images. It is this capacity that arises in the young child at this point and becomes his "work." In this way he comes to identify and build for himself a purposive outlook with the possibility of actively engaging life in a meaningful direction. It would be a pastoral *faux pas* if the Christian symbols were denied him on the grounds that he did not have this capacity.

Perhaps everyone has his own interpretation of that passage in the Gospels where Jesus tells his disciples to allow the little children to come to him. Joachim Jeremias, a contemporary German New Testament scholar, considers it a story told to support infant baptism. I find a certain psychological insight there. Our Lord is reported to have said: "I tell you, whoever does not accept the kingdom of God like a child will never enter it" (Mark 10:15). Certainly when we look for the unique capacity of the child we should include the freedom of imagination that can take an experience for what it is and will allow for the possibilities it offers. Revelation requires this of those who would be drawn into the being of God.

Fourth, there is the existential reason. At no time in a person's life does the family meal carry such important symbolic value as it does to the child of four or five. It is a feeling that is carried over into the birthday party, the festive family gatherings (recall how you felt when there was no room for you at the table when relatives came for Christmas or Thanksgiving), and the occasional visit to a formal restaurant. Part of the misbehavior associated with these events and small children is often the result of the excitement over the experience.

Children a little older—even as young as nine or ten—become preoccupied with events outside the immediate family, for which they push aside the family meal. Television, football, school programs, and various projects occupy a more important place for them. Having children in this age bracket, I can personally testify to the diminishing importance of the dining room table to my family—in spite of my preoccupation with its theoretical significance.

Related to this is the fifth item, the social reason. For a child in an expanding world there is the possibility of a more unified experience when there is a common symbol shared in his family life and then, as he becomes more aware of a wider community, in his church life. There is no break in flow from the family table, with all that can mean for him, and the parish altar, with its possible symbolic value.

Needless to say, adults have to act on the basis of the central significance of these symbols in home and church for the child to identify with them. A family that eats in front of the television set is going to have just as little possibility of awakening this latent symbolism as is the parish church where Morning Prayer is the custom or where the children under eight are relegated to a diet of "children's services." There is nothing automatic about the possibility of this transition, but with sensitivity it can be made most effectively at this period of development as it cannot at a later time. Then the chance for transitional experience, which is the foundation of learning, is lost.

The Symbol and The Role of Reason

But let the reader beware; for, as I promised, this chapter must end with a very important warning. Nothing said herein should be interpreted as advocating an anti-rationalism. Appeals to experience and the need to be aware of our feeings, to let the imagination work, are often interpreted as denigrating reason. On the contrary, it is just as sub-human never to move beyond felt meaning to a conceptualized form of experience and the images evoked within imagination and insight, as it is to think we can begin and end a meaningful life on the level of abstract judgments.

Formal operational thinking, i.e. the testing of hypotheses and the relating of conceptual judgments to one another, serves a necessary function in man. We cannot say that we know something until this process takes place, for responsible knowing requires clarity and community. Anyone who only lives on the level of experience is either limited to action based upon his individual exposure and fickle emotions or he becomes the slave of someone else's judgments. Rational thought sharpens our understanding and enables us to share in a logical way the judgments of others. Therefore, through it we have a much sounder basis for responsible action.

Many of us are familiar with the experience of going to a party, staying late, drinking a little too much, and saying and doing things which in the cold light of morning we regret. At the time of the party we did not talk over our action with our wife or husband and we did not really "think it through." The next morning at the breakfast table, in the presence of our spouse, we do both. We share and we clarify, which is what I mean by conceptual thinking. Lacking this, our actions were something short of responsible, that is, "appropriate to the situation in the light of our best judgment."

If the act of Holy Communion is a living symbol it must lead to action. For that action to be responsible it must ultimately emerge through the process of experience, imagination, insight, and judgment. This is true of all symbols and it is true of all growing-up. Adolescence is a time not just for new experiences but, far more important, it is a time for reflecting upon all our experiences to date. A real sign of maturity, according to Erik Erikson—his "eighth stage," which carries the virtue of wisdom—is the ability to reflect upon the experience of our parents who may now be long dead, and forgive them their wrongs and thank God for their strengths. Many of us never reach this stage, and most of us do not reach it until old age. Conceptual thought is not simultaneous with experience, but it needs to follow.

To recall Bellah's "symbolic realism," the important thing in the fulfillment of man's quest for meaning is that he find within his world symbols that can convey it. The Holy Communion is such a primal symbol, and it can cut through the confusion of a pluralistic culture such as our own. The problem lies in leading the person as early as possible to participation in such a symbol at the hands of an understanding community. It is to that end that the balance of this book is devoted.

CHAPTER 3

The Family and the Child's Communion

There seem to be two very conflicting notions abroad. One is that the family is dead, and the other is that the only possibility for religious meaning left us is the family. I am reminded of a similarly puzzling riddle of several years back: "There is no God and Mary is his mother!"

The family is not dead; it is perhaps in trouble. But even to say that, we need to qualify what we mean. Because one out of four marriages ends in divorce, it is not too difficult to conclude that an institution as old as man is about to collapse. It is quite easy to give the impression that when one cultural form of the family passes, the fundamental function of shaping the human person within the environment no longer exists. The obvious truth is that babies are born into social relationships of an immediate kind, which do inevitably become the context for a developing sense of self, and such a context defines what I mean by the social family.

There is no doubt that there are "good" families and "bad" families. How we might make such a value judgment is as debatable as any other ethical issue. Certainly it would relate to the end product's ability to cope as a future adult. My argument here will be that even more important is its ability to equip the person to engage in religious meaning, to be open to transcendence, and to possess the imagination and creativity that a symbol system (i.e., a coherent way of seeing life's meaning) requires of us.

Many things that are happening to the family are the result of the obvious rapid change within our culture. The institution does not have the support of a wider, homogeneous society, where a certain style of family life is unquestionably the logical thing. In the latter part of the nineteenth century in Western culture the patriarchal structure—in which father ruled and earned the living, mother kept the home and maintained a certain tone of resigned compassion before the lecherous old tyrant, and the children were seen (occasionally) and not heard—was taken for granted. We are light years away from those times.

Our divorce rate is an indication of several things. One of them is certainly the fact that a marriage must now find its strength from within. The society will not demand of it a specific conformity. It is also an indication of our style of mate selection. In a highly mobile society, persons are liable to marry for largely emotional reasons, some conscious and many unconscious, rather than for reasons of economic or social expedience. But there is also the simple fact that where an early death, particularly of the mother in childbirth, resolved many an unhappy union a hundred years ago, we now have a more humane solution: divorce. My great-grandfather, a Methodist circuit-rider whom his children charitably described as a "hard man," married three times—twice before he was thirty.

One clear indication of our need not to make facile judgments about the shape of the "good" family has been the reaction to the Moynihan report on the black family in the ghetto. It abstracted all kinds of conclusions as to the cause of ghetto crime on the criteria of the "bad" condition of black families. Scholars such as Robert Coles have, on the other hand, insisted that different styles of family life are not necessarily bad because they do not conform; and, in fact, the so-called absent black father is in reality no more "absent" from his children than the white, suburban father who commutes to the city.

Undoubtedly family styles may change. The Israeli experiments with the *kibbutz* are very different from the isolated, nuclear family (consisting of two generations, parents and children), which Talcott Parsons tells us is so appropriate for industrial America. Recent studies testify to the strength of the *kibbutzim* in producing happy, creative people. The communes in rural as well as other areas of America and the multi-sexual relationships seriously advanced by the so-called "swingers" might both be indicative of a groping toward the future. Herbert Richardson, in *Nun, Witch, Playmate* argues for the dawning in man of a kind of poly-consciousness that gives a theoretical, theological base for just this style of family life.

I would say that, given the problems we all feel in determining what the family of the future might be like and how we might so structure our mate selection to avoid the misery that afflicts much married life today, the truth is that the family is as important today as it ever has been for man. Gibson Winter some years ago spoke of the family as a "covenant of intimacy." This is to say that it is both the source and the means of acquiring that depth of relationship without which we become in fact "hollow men" in a technological age.

Thomas Luckmann in *The Invisible Religion* has more recently argued that the symbolic universe which makes up our grasp of ultimate meaning can extend today no further than the family. There is no possibility, he believes, in a pluralistic, heterogeneous, socio-cultural reality of one "sacred canopy" or "cosmos," one way of understanding God and his ways with man.

It would almost seem that we are returning to the religious world of the early Roman Republic, where every family had its own gods and the marriage rite (on which our present customs are so heavily dependent) consisted of the bride rejecting the gods of her father for the gods of her husband. Certainly the Roman family was bigger than our contemporary nuclear family; and I would argue that if Luckmann is right, his thesis applies to something a little larger than the two-generation, parent-child, relationship. Perhaps it is more like the band of fifty, for which I spoke in *The Future Shape of Ministry* and now find has an ethological base in the hunting band common to 99 percent of man's history. But be that as it may, we have become aware in just the last few years of the absolutely central role of the family in shaping the religious consciousness of the individual.

The child's preparation for Holy Communion takes place almost exclusively in the family, whether we intend that or not. This is not a matter so much of his immediate, conscious preparation, but, far more important, his long range preparation from the moment of birth. The possibility of a child "discerning the Lord's body" depends on what happens in the family from the moment of his birth (and maybe even before) to the time of his first communion—and then beyond. It is absolutely essential that the reader understand this and banish from his mind any notion that I am going to present a "neat little program" that is going to do the trick in a few hours before the day of the child's communion. There are programs to help you and your child focus what has happened in your life together to that date and to indicate how this points to your sacramental relationship with God. I shall speak of those at the end of the next chapter. But the major task before us now, and before all parents, is the over-all preparation, which is a matter of years and our total style of life.

The Central Role of the Family

If you will pardon this Jesuit-trained Episcopalian, their old saying was intuitively correct: "Give us the child until he is seven and he is ours for life." This belief has received substantial documentation in the work of Benjamin Bloom (*Stability and Change in Human Characteristics*), who argues that the "macro-personality" (the term is mine), the basic shape of the self, is developed by age five. Intelligence, sexuality, linguistic ability, self-esteem, trust, disposition and prevailing mood, intellectual interests, and so forth are the result of the individual's genetic type in dialogue with his environment before he ever gets to grade school.

This runs very contrary to thoughts that personality change is equally available to us throughout life if a powerful enough agent is brought to bear. Popularly this notion has expressed itself in the fear of the parents of adolescents, who stand trembling before the prospect of what the "outside world" might do to their children now leaving home. In our fantasies we imagine that all kinds of bad influences might destroy the value system which we have worked for fourteen, sixteen, or even eighteen years to build. What Bloom and others believe is that what our child carries into his adolescent life and beyond is very much determined by what happened to him during those years before he ever entered the first grade.

Fitzhugh Dodson, author of *How To Parent,* reinforces this in saying to parents: "The most important thing your baby acquires during this stage of infancy [from birth until he walks] is his *basic outlook on life.* He is forming, from a baby's point of view, his philosophy of life." I hope it is evident from everything that I have said to this point that Dodson is talking about the child's potentiality for a religious life, his openness to revelation, and his freedom to act on the basis of a faith in God revealed in Christ. This aptly explains why I insist that the family has always been central; it is particularly so now.

This insight has been the source for much reflection by theologians such as Gabriel Moran. Moran has said repeatedly that revelation should be understood as God's presence to us in the total experience of life, and that religious education is the development of a method of theological reflection that conceptualizes, clarifies, and shares this experience. The latter is an adult function. The experience of God belongs to all ages, and it is through this that we are formed. There is, therefore, a great need to distinguish between education and formation.

It is possible to create a kind of dichotomy in which the task of the institutional Church is to educate and the task of the family is to form, and in fact this is more or less my thesis. The family is primarily the source of formation (the shaping of personality), and education does go on in the parish church (or should), as we shall discuss in the next chapter. But the institutional Church also has a responsibility to serve the family in the task of formation, and we need to avoid giving the impression that this is something each family does in complete isolation from a larger body.

This service should most appropriately be to assist the parents in developing a sensitivity to the ways in which a child's religious formation takes place. It means a willingness not to be "in control" and to work toward an understanding of ministry that is less neat than the professional models often presented us. This is difficult in a technological culture, where manipulation of the environment is a goal constantly held before us. In fact, parents expect answers of the clergy, not the kind of call to participation and discovery that is held up to us by the counterculture in turning away from a technological society.

What needs to happen in the dialogue between parents and priest is a realization of the significance of a cognition Jerome Bruner calls "thinking of the left hand." He sets this over and against "thinking of the right hand"—which is logical, analytical, and rational—as a kind of intuitive, imaginative, and "hunchy" thinking. Somewhere we must find the courage to take such forms of thought seriously—just as seriously as the analytical mode—for not only does art and literature emerge from "thinking of the left hand," but so does religion. This is not to deny the necessity for logical, analytical thought, but to insist that what we want is a dialogic relationship between the two in all our lives.

I once outlined the distinction between these two kinds of thought in a talk to a group of churchmen.

Among them was the father of a high-school senior who announced that he did not want to go to college right away but would like to take a year or so off just to "think." For the father, the connection he made between what his son wanted to do and "thinking of the left hand" was a very liberating discovery. It made sense and he liked it.

Intuitive thinking is communicated and learned in very subtle ways. It is something acquired early or not at all, as the young child senses the tone of our voice, the expression on our face, our posture, the rooms we live in, the way we treat one another, our attitude toward our body, what we hang on our walls, how we change a diaper or discover a "wet bed," what we do with our leisure, the music we enjoy, our use of nature, our knowledge of art, our enjoyment of food, and many more things. Often it is very difficult for us to grasp just what is the texture of our family life *vis-a-vis* the "thinking of the left hand," to discover what possibilities there are for our children to discern what the English poet, Gerard Manley Hopkins, called the *inscape* of life. He meant by this the inner nature of a thing, the essence which leads us inevitably to the source of its creation in God, as opposed to the *landscape* that is the description of the "outside."

I would suggest that there is no more important task for young Christian parents today than to examine the possibilities within their own family life for the perception of Hopkins' *inscape*. It is not something we can attack head on, because intuitive or imaginative thinking grows on the margin of the organized and the structured life and is not susceptible to the American problem-solving approach. No computer, no systems analysis, no efficiency engineer can provide a program guaranteed to produce a family open to revelation. It is a matter of how we live. Somehow it involves being with persons who live with some very suggestive "loose ends," unfinished or uncontrolled. It is a matter of learning to expect the unexpected.

How do we go about discovering how this might happen in a family? It would seem to me that in all our contemporary work in laboratory groups and their examination of the lived experience, there ought to be some way of developing what I call the "anti-therapy group" (if I may define "therapy" as a means of assisting someone in finding his place in a defined socio-cultural structure). In anti-therapy the function of the imagination and the exploration of the mystery of the *inscape* of life would be encouraged. The communication theorists talk about the need to "meta-communicate," to talk about what we mean to be saying in order that our meaning might be more precise. Can we as a family and together with other families "meta-communicate" about our "thinking of the left hand," so that we can encourage not the preciseness of our communication, but its translucence?

A religious consciousness demands a sense of mystery. A family life in which there is no sense of mystery—be it talk of fairies, Santa Claus, and the Easter Bunny or the Trinity, Incarnation, and Grace—strangles the religious potential of the child. He goes through life mentally retarded on the "left hand," incapable of that wonder akin to madness (which R. D. Laing says is the root of the sense of transcendence). If he ever "gets religion," his pursuit of God is as clumsy as would be the efforts of a computer programmed to write the *Confessions of St. Augustine.*

Symbolic Patterns of Family Living

What happens in a family begins with what is communicated between the husband and wife. If marriage is two individuals who meet occasionally for "sex" (that is, the mutual or not-so-mutual release of tension), the organization of a household, and the care for the material needs of the children, then we have very little to go on. Such a marriage amounts to no more than a legal contract permitting a certain contact between the *landscape* of each person, without any possible engagement of the respective *inscapes*.

My initial assumption is that what we want and potentially have is more than this. We do "enter into" one another in a way that our physical expression of that phrase is symbolic of the sharing of our total selves. Our initial task is to identify the symbols of that relationship in order to understand the possibilities which it grounds for our children. I am speaking of the very profound realities as well as some very simple things, both of which open for us the wonder of the marriage.

Obviously we begin with the mystery of sexual play, its excitement from the first tingle of suggestion to the ecstasy of orgasm. The conjugal bed and the dining table, across which we experience the joy and the intangible "something" found in that shared meal, form the two symbol-objects that are most evocative in a marriage. A house that does not provide for a "sacred space" for these does not have the possibility for me of becoming a real home. Any list of symbols might also include "our song," the old sofa bought from initial savings, the painting "we had to have," and the "stupid" little sayings we conjured up to express our love (the very sounds, if not their meanings, evoke a feeling of the shared mystery). My wife and I have some scrapbooks that include, among other treasures, the cork from the champagne we once drank with the French Consul-General, a rose we bought in a South Philadelphia restaurant, and a program from an opera I loved and she slept through. Why keep them? Because they have the power of meaning!

Symbols constitute meaning. A shared meaning requires a common symbolic system. A creative marriage needs a solid foundation in those mutual values, derived from a shared meaning. It is not the thing-in-itself which conveys the power of a symbol, but how we use it to open ourselves to the mystery of the other person. Bread and wine—even the exotic kind we use at the Holy Eucharist—are simply things in themselves, but between God and his Church they open up great meaning and make accessible values that have changed the world. They are a means of revelation to the communicant that comes with an imagination, and therefore are further examples of the symbols already found in marriage.

But the training of such an imagination begins with a man and woman who will not be satisfied with the surface phenomena, with a world reduced to a *landscape*. It requires the tempering of the logical and analytical existence, with the spontaneous and the intuitive life. In such a relationship, where the latter has its play, the symbols of those shared lives become naturally evident in a way that excites the imagination.

There are symbols of marriage which belong to the couple alone, and others become equally the property of the children. The loving touch, the kiss, the embrace that the parents share before the child and that communicate to him the ineffable delight of his parents' relationship, overflow to the child himself. They become the symbols that draw him into the mystery of that love which undergirds and transcends the anger, the anxiety, and the guilt that are part of growing up. My youngest son, from the time he could walk until he reached the age of ten, whenever he saw his mother and me hug one another, crawled up in the middle of the embrace. This seems to me not just the response of an envious boy going through some kind of Oedipal crisis, but a joy in sharing this delightful expression of love.

Furthermore, it is important for a child to see that his parents hold "things" dear, not as some kind of crass materialism but because they embody for them a past and communicate a present that enables them to look to the future with hope. This brings us to a delicate point where our latter-day Puritanism puts us in the position of opposing "things" and "persons." There is nothing in what I am saying which suggests that parents should choose material possessions over personal relationships. The child no more takes second place to these than we take second place to the Sacraments in the eyes of God. The issue at hand is that we do not know one another, we do not experience the other, apart from a symbolic world. This means a world of things and events charged with meaning. I am suggesting that we as parents need to divest ourselves of frugality-for-frugality's-sake, bad art in the name of practicality, and a guilt complex about our pet indulgences (which can be one person's name for another person's symbol). The kinds of sacrifices we need to talk about are those of going into debt to travel, to buy good art, or to play.

For it is in terms of these events and things that the family finds the joy that draws them together and, consequently, opens them to God's self-disclosure.

Of course, a labored self-consciousness about such family symbols becomes precious and boring. It is like walking through a house decorated solely by the interior decorator from Neiman-Marcus. While it can be exquisite, it is also cold and empty "good taste." The symbols of which I speak arise spontaneously as we become free to enjoy our world, and they are therefore in a certain sense covert.

There comes a time, however, when we need to pursue *overtly* the symbolic life of the family. I might note here, in passing, several excellent guides to doing just this: Dolores Curran, *Who Me Teach My Children Religion?* (Winston Press); Fitzhugh Dodson, *How To Parent* (Signet); and a book that at first sight may appear quite unlikely, Northrop Frye, *The Educated Imagination* (Indiana University Press). Some people might find Christiane Brusselmans and Edward Wakin, *A Parent's Guide: Religion for Little Children* (Our Sunday Visitor Publications) a good resource, although it is more obviously Roman Catholic in orientation. For guidance in family worship, Gabe Huck, *A Book of Family Prayer*, and Ed Hays, *Prayers for the Domestic Church: A Handbook for Worship in the Home* are helpful. Tilden Edwards, *Sabbath Time* (Seabury), has useful insights into mealtime rituals. Nursery and kindergarten materials from such publishers as Silver Burdett, The Seabury Press, William H. Sadlier, Morehouse-Barlow, and Winston Press, can also be helpful.

The conscious pursuit of symbols of our life together starts with family rituals. I will say more about this in the next section, but for now I would call attention to two parts of a young family's life that naturally evoke a ritual. If we remember that a ritual is a collection of symbols and that symbols convey the inner meaning of our relationship to one another and God, then we can keep in mind what all this is about.

The first area evocative of a ritual treatment is bedtime. Dodson, as a psychologist, say that bedtime should be carried out as a ritual following a definite, repetitive form. John G. Williams in a very helpful book now out of print, *Worship and the Modern Child,* adds that from the very time a baby comes home from the hospital the parents should kneel at his crib to say their prayers, and that this should progress as a part of regular routine of the child's life as he grows older. In this way he is constantly reminded of the relationship of his parents, to whom he looks for everything, to God upon whom both they and he are dependent.

By the bedtime ritual, however, I do not mean just bedtime prayers. The ritual would include a prescribed time, a warm cuddling, a changing of dress and washing, perhaps a snack, and, most important, the reading of a story. The need to read to our children cannot be emphasized enough. It becomes the food of their imagination. At what stage we read what is open to debate. Dodson's book contains an exhaustive catalogue broken down by age. Certainly stories that awaken and stimulate the imagination are the most important. Frye insists that it should begin with the Bible and move on to the Classics, inasmuch as they are the source of our imaginative heritage. Needless to say, however, we do not read chunks of the Bible or even the classics to little children; these require considerably more developed intellectual capacities than children possess. Doing this we do more damage than good. (Ronald Goldman,

Readiness for Religion [Seabury], provides an analysis of this issue.) Yet it may well be possible to share with small children the more imaginative folk tales and colorful characters from the Bible that do not require theological reflection to grasp and do not "hang them up" in a primitive notion of God.

Speaking for myself, my fondest memories of early childhood are of my mother reading to me at bedtime from *Winnie-the-Pooh* and *Wind in the Willows*. I always regretted that my own children never seemed to enjoy them as I; but just the other day my seventeen-year-old daughter was recalling with delight her own bedtime with us and then progressively our younger three children. For the life of me I cannot remember what we read, but she has been reading ever since. She lives in a world of all kinds of people, many of whom she has only met in books. Her younger sister has a delightful fantasy world all of her own. So it must have somehow been right.

The other area susceptible to ritual formation is mealtime. I have already stated my belief that the dining table is one of the two most important pieces of furniture in a house. I would now add that the TV set must be removed, if at all possible, out of eyesight and earshot. TV trays and TV dinners are unmentionable! Aim for quality of family meals, and avoid running your kitchen like a "short-order hash-house." What every family needs is a time when all the family sits down at the dinner table several times a week and leisurely shares good food and one another.

Obviously this experience becomes in some ways more significant as the children grow older. But my own conviction is that as soon as a child can sit reasonably well he ought to be at table with his parents and siblings. If the tone of the whole affair is less than subdued—it is a favorite time for pitched battles in our family—I am not sure this is all bad. One of the problems in many American families is that we never meet one another on deep enough levels to have anything to fight about. The point is that this eating together is our familial "sacred meal" where we find unity in one another and in God. No activity, no ringing of the telephone, no irresistible TV program or book should stand in the way of this sacramental event. It can happen, if we believe it is important enough.

The relevant point for this book is that the unity found in the family meal leads us on to the basic symbol of the Eucharist itself. The bridge between the two is marked by the Grace said at meals. While the father is the "priest" of the family, and he appropriately presides, I see no reason why he cannot delegate this task to others in the family. My own children have often vied for the opportunity. Even if in the actual saying of the Grace a certain spirit of devotion is lacking, it would appear to me that prayer at this time is the barest minimum for a Christian family and is basic to the experience of prayer in the larger family at the parish church.

Beyond these two ritualized dimensions of family action, I would point out that the space which the family occupies needs to be one that appreciates beauty. I am personally convinced that one of the grimmest defects of the Puritan culture, under which we still struggle, is the divorcement of the good from the beautiful and the consequent implication that to be concerned for art, music, drama, and literature is to be frivolous or impractical or both. The result of pushing art to the periphery of our life is the impoverishment of our imagination and life's meaning.

Our living space defines us. When I speak to the students in my classes about parish calling, I always tell them to look around the home in which they are visiting. The walls, the bookshelves, the tables, and the furniture in the room offer a good insight into the character of the people upon whom they are calling. I have found this true myself, and I think it takes very little effort on their part to develop this sensitivity.

In saying this to groups whom I have addressed on this subject, I am not infrequently met by the comment, "I would never let you make a parish call!" That is beside the point, even if true. We are speaking of the children whose imagination is shaped by what they perceive in the home, what they read and what they hear. This is not a simple matter of an objective transcendence of taste, but the climate of feeling built up as the viewing subject interprets the expressions or indications of the others' life in the "living space." Sometimes this interpretation can result in a swing to an opposite symbolic expression (e.g., from a fondness for plush Victorian to very simple contemporary). People cannot, however, avoid what their "living space" says to them, and this relates very directly to their religion. We all need to share, then, a sensitivity to the symbolic function of the home surroundings.

In addition to this, it needs to be emphasized that the little child ought to be encouraged to contribute on his own to what is to be seen and heard in that home. The pictures he draws can very well be put up, if not in the living room, certainly in the family room or the kitchen. His records should not be relegated to the $29.98 player in his room, on which one sounds just like the other—a noisy screech. And he should be taken to the local library and enjoined to read with the family the kind of books that interest him as well as those that concern his parents.

The involvement of the child in the family's literary and artistic life on his level leads us on to the matter of play. As I have indicated, one way of understanding liturgy is as play, and if the person is to live happily with this creative notion, then he needs to learn as a little child that play is important and something we all do. Therefore, the parents ought to play with their children. I am not saying that they ought to play at not being parents and assume the role of a "buddy," but as parents, who are also playing human beings, they need to share in the child's play world.

There are many games we can all play, and some even little children enjoy. How many countless sessions of "Fish" have my wife and I participated in? There is something very healthy in getting down on the floor and tumbling with our children, playing with their ball or truck, or doing a little "let's pretend." I would suggest a measure of caution in the roughhouse kind of play. My older son's clearest memory of our every-evening "football game" on the living room rug when he was about four was the time I flipped him over and knocked the wind out of him. Despite such accidents, the general tone of all this kind of activity is quite religious because, in playing, our hope for the future can take on the kind of reality in which it becomes a vivid possibility. Somehow despair, a preoccupation with the mistakes of the past and the frustrations of the present moment, passes when we can play at some new image of the future. Here emerge new symbols or old ones now more powerful in our life.

Family Life as a Dramatic System

The point has been made by some social scientists that aside from the social system of institutions and roles and the cultural system of concepts and logic, there is something in human communities called the *dramatic system.* This is a dimension of life which weaves through the passage of time as a persistent, colorful thread. It is "the golden cord, close binding all mankind" (*Hymnal* 263). We perceive it neither functionally nor logically, but aesthetically.

C. S. Lewis in his autobiography describes something which he calls "joy," an aspect of life interwoven within the mundane affairs of common sense, which in truth gives a reason for living and was for him the experience of conversion. The late Abraham Maslow, a psychologist, seems to me to have sought a scientific understanding of much the same phenomenon in describing "peak experiences," occasions when our consciousness is broadened or we come to a new level of awareness. "Joy" or "peak experiences," whatever it is called, is the experience of transcendence which *changes* us. In many communities and families they are found in a kind of dramatic dimension which opens us to the recurring possibility of experiencing the mystery of God.

Such come particularly in the celebration of special events. Birthdays, anniversaries, graduations, and similar occasions are a private part of a family's dramatic system. National celebrations and, more important, celebrations of the Church year are a public part of the same drama in which each family works out its own private expression. Jack Lundin in a book called *Cele-*

brations for Special Days and Occasions (Harper and Row) attempts to provide a resource for this purpose, and while it comes off in a rather "canned" and artificial manner, certainly his intention is to be warmly commended. Perhaps some people might find the material there helpful.

What needs to be grasped is the principle underlying what I and Lundin support. It is as if we lived in two times, one sacred and the other profane. Religion "works" by engaging us in a dialogic process between the two times, and as we pass from one to the other we are refreshed to meet the world of common sense anew and, at the same time, challenged to demand of our religion a spirit which speaks to our condition. This is quite different from living a kind of schizoid existence, where the sacred and profane never meet, or from existing only in a religious ghetto or in the two-dimensional world of common sense. The power lies in the dialogue between the dramatic system and the other two, the cultural and social systems.

What do we do in our families with Advent? Christmas? Lent? Easter? As my own children grow older I have noticed that "going to church" has become for them an ever greater chore, but God forbid that we should light the Advent candle when one of them is absent! I realize that Christmas trees can be a great nuisance. I myself get a secret delight in this throwback to pagan northern European ancestors; but over and above my private pleasure and even with the family fights over which tree we get, there is a wonder in the smell and sight of the lighted tree that is nowhere else duplicated for us. As I get older and reflect on what brought me to the priesthood, among many other things it was the ability of my father on these great celebrations to introduce me and my sisters to a world of wonder and mystery that called me on to explore and share its meaning.

It is very difficult to describe in three easy steps *how* a family truly celebrates sacred time in its own dramatic system. It is like telling someone how to study the paintings in an art gallery or how to appreciate the beauty of nature. It grows by doing it. I would say that the main thing is not to neglect these occasions. That peculiar form of self-conscious Western masculinity that thinks it is funny for the husband to forget his wedding anniversary, unmanly to remember his children's birthdays, and perfectly natural to be too busy to do anything more on Christmas than run out the day before and "get his old lady something," is not only indicative of something emotionally unscrewed, it also impoverishes life! We need to use our imagination to incorporate the family's style of life in an imaginative way into a life of celebration (including the celebration of our sins).

I am often asked, in this regard, whether or not I consider Santa Claus, the Easter Bunny, and the "tooth fairy" un-Christian. There are those who think that the child confuses such stories with the Gospel or anything else his parents tell him that is true (that is, accepted by the adult consensus of the culture), and therefore he is confused as to what to believe or ends up concluding that his parents are liars. I suppose that there are cases of this, but I have never encountered them. It smacks of a kind of dull literalism, which gives little credit to the perception of children and assumes that adults have an easy access to the truth. I personally feel that the letter in the New York *Sun*, "Yes, Virginia, There Is a Santa Claus," is more than a sentimental, heart warming part of our past. It is—quite unintentionally, I am sure—a rather insightful analysis of the *nature of knowing*.

I might add that while I personally recognize the abuse in the commercialization of Christmas, I also am very suspicious of the incipient Puritanism in America. I get the feeling that some of the "get-Christ-back-in-Christmas" crowd would just love to run up and down the streets crying, "No Christmas tonight!" That to me is an abomination.

One further word on the subject of sacred time is in order. Part of such existence is birth at one end and death at the other. Young children ought in some way to be aware of both. This does not mean thrusting either upon them in a manner in which they are incapable of understanding, any more than hiding either one on the theory that they are too sensitive. For almost all of man's history young children have viewed the birth of their younger siblings and have watched their elders die. Is the problem that children are now more easily undone, or is it that adults have not worked through their feelings on this matter? At the very minimum, I think that little children should not be cut off from the beginning and end of the life cycle of their pets and should be allowed to celebrate their birth and death in their own rituals. I also think it is most advisable that children not only witness baptisms, but also funerals (assuming that the latter are not merely the unartful display of the mortician's skill). For in these rituals we probe the greatest mysteries implicit in death and birth.

The Immediate Preparation of the Child

I am almost at the end of this chapter and only now do I come to the subject you might have thought would be the principal object of my discussion. Yet with a little reflection maybe you would agree with me that if we have done well what I have discussed up to this point, and if as a family we are participating in our parish church (which I shall speak of in the next chapter), then we might expect that there would come a time when our child would spontaneously express a desire to make his communion. It may not come in just so many words. We need to listen to our children sometimes and be aware of how very sensitive they are to even our nonverbal reservations about this kind of thing. I have had parents assure me that their children were "just as happy with a blessing," when it seemed to me that every time I passed them at the altar they much preferred to share with the rest of us.

When this time of wanting to partake does come, our hope would be that it follows naturally from their family life in relation to their parish church life. The Roman Catholic stipulation is that a child is "ready" when he knows the difference between the Eucharist and his family meal. I am not that interested in emphasizing the "difference," but rather the natural sequence of symbols. The decision as to *when,* as Francis Buckley in *Children and God* (Corpus) says for Roman Catholics, is undoubtedly up to the parents and the child, not the parish priest. The priest should only advise, because this is an event growing out of the family life and its particular style. For this reason, no arbitrary age should be set; although without doubt what others do will influence the feelings of all the children in the parish.

Once the decision is made within the family for a child to make his communion, the immediate preparation is up to the parents. I think those parishes that have "copped out" on this are losing a great deal! No one but the parents knows what there is to build on in each child's experience, and it is rightly and invariably different in each case. If we reduce the preparation to a "mini-confirmation class," then we lose much of the natural order of symbols that I have discussed in this chapter.

The task of the parents in the immediate preparation is simply to focus with the child on the meaning of the symbol of the communion as it relates to God in Christ in terms of the symbols the child has experienced in his family life. There is no special number of sessions and the less formally this is done (which is *not* to say the more unstructured) the better. If the child has no religious imagination, then the whole exercise is futile and we can expect what religious life he has as he grows older to be on the order of magic. After several encounters with so-called "Jesus freaks," I suspect most of them suffered from a severe retardation of the religious imagination. Our hope is that the understanding at the level at which the child is will be part of a natural flow, in which he focuses all that he has experienced and learned of the mystery of God on this act of communion.

The parish may well provide a supportive instruction for the parents and materials to use with the children. Certainly both are most helpful, and I would encourage participation as a great learning opportunity for adults. It then follows that it is to this supportive role of the parish that we now need to move, in the desire to see just what can be done on the larger scale to undergird both this immediate preparation and, more generally, the whole of the life of the young family.

CHAPTER 4

The Parish and Children's Communions

Mary Douglas has suggested that in a society such as our own, where there is little emphasis upon the structuring of the individual's thought process and where families are more egalitarian and personal than hierarchically ordered there is a likelihood that neat discriminations in religious thought and highly predictable cultic action will break down. We no longer burn or exile people if their ideas do not conform. We may think them strange and, if their skin is a different color, we might discriminate against them; but on the whole we tolerate a measure of independent thinking. We may also rail against "permissivism" in the contemporary family, but no one has the time or energy to attempt to do much about it. So in our parish churches the clergy find themselves with less and less to say that they know for certain is right, and we fight the battles of liturgical change with little hope that in the foreseeable future order will emerge out of the chaos.

As I visit various areas of the Church it seems to me that much of the anxiety about this focuses itself on the whole new order of baptism, first communion, and confirmation. What we have been doing for many centuries in the English Church makes no historical or theological sense. This statement may sound a little extreme and I cannot defend it here. Beyond what I have said about it in chapter two, I would refer the reader to a "conversation" in April, 1972, issue of *The Anglican Theological Review*. This article could be the nucleus of a parish study group or a clerical gathering, for it explains why we followed the old order and why it makes no sense. But whether or not it can be defended, the previous sequence of baptism, confirmation, and first communion was what we were used to and it was comfortable. In fact, it appears to me that much of the parish's program was formed about this cycle, and little that the Episcopal Church has done in the way of change has gone so far to upset the accustomed way of doing things as this rearrangement.

We are faced now with a whole new way within the parish to structure the nurturing of God's people in Christ. Undoubtedly this can be disturbing, but also it can open to us opportunities to guide the future of the Church's parish life in a way that reflects a deeper understanding of how people develop in religion. For example, at its meeting at Pocono in Pennsylvania in the Fall of 1971, the House of Bishops discussed the need for confirmation as a "rite of passage." It is my belief that the statement which resulted from this discussion can be questioned both theologically and historically, but the point is that at least we are trying to deal with the relation of the Church's action to the developmental cycle of the person. This is something new and it is very important. If we take it seriously, it will mean that the ministry of the parish community will be greatly altered for two reasons. First, because the developmental cycle of the person as he moves from infant to child to adolescent to adult is a function, in

part, of the culture, and we have been living off cultural
patterns now dead. Second, because much of what we
have done in the past (such as demanding confirmation
before communion) has been the result of historical
expediency, and those situations have long passed.

It must be said at the beginning that there is a pastoral necessity in reordering our parish life not to
"alienate the faithful." There are plenty of people who
could not care less about history or theology, and who
come to their church for support in a very anxious
world. A friend of mine, an active layman, recently
wrote to his bishop in a letter published in the diocesan
newspaper, that "Christian charity for honest confusion, doubt, and perplexity seems strangely lacking in
both the hierarchy and the parochial clergy." His plea
is that we comfort people, not afflict them with "novel-
ties" and "relevance."

Certainly we can appreciate what is being said and
perhaps the parish priest can begin by sharing his own
discomfort in an uncertain world not of his own making. There is a measure of therapy (and that is what is
being requested) in his *transparent* self, which is to
say: letting his own emotional life show. (For those
who are interested in pursuing this statement, Sidney
M. Jourard's book, *The Transparent Self: Self-Disclosure and Well-Being* [Van Nostrand] is a good introduction.) But we must not ignore the warning of those
social scientists who predict that ecclesiastic function
solely centered on therapy is doomed to a slow demise.
More and more anthropologists remind us that the
function of religion centers in the dialogic relationship
between the symbolic world of personal change and
the structured, immediate world of common sense. The
latter happens in our time to be a cause of much

anxiety. The familiar patterns are shaken, and consequently we often look to our religion to assure us of the old truths. But a vital religion will, on the contrary, demand of us something new, and will send us into the world of common sense not just reassured, but changed. My conviction is that the parish church must always operate within that understanding.

The Focus of the Community's Ministry

Ministry is the service of the Church, the primal sacrament of Christ. It is the action of the parish community, not the description of the rector or vicar's role. We simply must break away from the notion, now many centuries old, that a parish is made up of the priest and his assistant priests who actively minister to a more or less passive congregation. Frances Young, lay ministries officer of the Executive Council, wrote a while ago in a supplement on lay ministry appearing in *The Episcopalian:* "The most exciting and alive parishes I visited were those which were 'learning communities,' where clergy and lay people together were sharing in planning and decision-making, in successes and in failures." I could not agree more with this statement, and would speculate here on how we might shape that learning of Christ together in the most effective manner.

For if we understand the baptism of the infant—and irrespective of what might be theoretically wisest the Episcopal Church is going to go on baptizing infants for the foreseeable future—to mean that he is fully initiated into Christ's Church, and if we accept what I have argued here as to the natural sequence of a child's admission to communion, then persons living the full sacramental life of the Church will come to adulthood *with the need to understand intellectually what their religious experience means.* I am assuming that, whatever the House of Bishops chooses to do, the practice of instruction and confirmation at the latter half of childhood will die. If this happens, it lays before us the naked reality of the need for adult education. This is because we will have no period between admission to communion at age four, five, six, or seven and the time of the assumption of adult responsibility in life where we think, rightly or wrongly, we are equipping churchmen for theological thought and adult responsibility as Christians.

Of course there is Sunday or Church School. But what function does this serve? John Westerhoff in *Values for Tomorrow's Children* has asked that question, and as a specialist in Christian education his answer is, "No function of real value." Reflecting on much the same data as I have in this book, he believes that we are wasting our time with religious education aimed at the six- to twelve-year-old (and certainly this is the main thrust of most formal Christian education), and that in its place we should have week-day schools for pre-school children and neighborhood groups for adult education (including the young people). Robert Neil and Michael O'Donovan have made much the same suggestion in a book on Roman Catholic education.

I am not quite so sure that I am willing to write off the educational programs of our parish churches for the six- to twelve-year-olds, if for no other reason than their need for a community religious experience *of which they feel a part.* I am more enthusiastic about Westerhoff's focus on little children and their parents. His emphasis on the value of nursery school and kindergarten also reinforces my own experience and what Dodson recommends in *How To Parent.* This means that the traditional Sunday School is peripheral, and that I believe is true.

But to pursue the positive elements in this argument, if we could imagine a paradigm of the family's life cycle, we would see that there is operative three generations (children, parents, grandparents), with a new generation coming into being at approximately every twenty to twenty-five years. In that cycle there is a period of about five to seven years where the grandparents are experiencing their children leaving home; the parents are courting and marrying, adjusting to one another, and living with young children; and the children are being born and experiencing the most formative years of their lives. All this is happening at once, all of it is particularly critical, and it appears to me to be that dimension of the family cycle upon which ministry needs to focus.

What I am seeking to do is answer a question which is very high on the priorities of many clergy. If we do away with confirmation instruction (granting that it never did the job), when do people learn what it is to be an adult, thinking Christian, making an adult decision for Christ? That is a very important question. My tentative answer is that beginning with just before marriage and running through the time in which they have small children, we need to have a series of structures in which the parish community involves these young adults in learning the means of theological reflection. By "structures" I mean such as the traditional pre-marital instruction (but far more than the one hour some clergy manage), the neighborhood catechetical groups suggested by Westerhoff, the post-marital parish

group I outline in *The Sexual Person,* the personal
ministry of the priest I shall discuss in the next section,
the Sunday morning adult discussion group so common
in many parishes, and the parents' group for preparing
children for communion. Undoubtedly there are other
possible structures we can imagine. (A very helpful introduction to some methodological guides for the development of these can be found in Howard Clinebell's
The People Dynamic [Harper & Row].)

What do we expect to have happen in these "structures?" Generally speaking, we are seeking to build a
community learning Christ, where the young child's
development toward communion is an integral part.
But more specifically I would list four essentials, without
which I do not think such a community can exist. First,
we should seek to clarify our experience. What is
happening to me, the young adult, in terms of my total
self (body, past, community, projects for the future)?
What is happening to my parents? What is or will be
happening to my children? Second, we need to develop
a consciousness of a natural group. Part of the basic
problem of parish ministry today is that it is built on
artificial groups, collections of people who have no
shared experience except a feeling that they *ought* to
have. We have to begin with *what is,* and here this is
our life together starting out in the business of shaping
a family. I believe adult catechesis always begins with
such a recognition of common experience. Third, we
must acquire the community memory. The tradition
of the Church, which includes the Bible, is the way in
which we in the past have clarified and shared our
experience of God in Christ for two thousand years.
Today we live out of our memory toward the future.
To try anything else is to substitute fantasy for imagina-

tion. Fourth, we have to learn the skills of theological reflection. To relate our experience, our life together, and our past in a way that can give meaning to the hope for union with God requires theological thinking. We ask what it all means. The answer lies in our ability to make judgments upon our insight into the presence of God in Christ in our lives now.

I am not offering here anything that has not been suggested in one place or another. What I hope I have done, however, is to have stated as baldly as I can what seems to me to be the primary focus of the kind of parish that takes seriously the revolutionary change so subtly advanced by *Prayer Book Studies 18* and that believes that the ministry of the Church is found in those communities that seek as one to learn Christ.

The Role of the Priest

There is a certain relief and a certain anxiety involved in saying to the rector or vicar, "It is no longer just up to you." For some time now we have felt the loneliness and the pressure of being expected to produce a successful program that made our people happy Christians. But we also have to admit that sometimes we have enjoyed the sense of omnipotence that comes with a successful illusion. This is particularly true if we have been able to surround ourselves with the presence of passive Christians, found in every area, whose peace depends on letting Father play at being God. But this will not do for our purposes.

In *The Future Shape of Ministry* and in "Transcendence and Ministry," an article in the January, 1972, issue of *The Anglican Theological Review* and reprinted in May, 1972, issue of *The Review for Religious,*

I have been developing a model of the priest's function as an *artist*. He is one who by his life and words seeks to evoke for people's imaginations the *inscape* of life. How does the priest assist in the parish's role in regard to the communion of its children? My answer would be, in some sense, as "God's artists in residence." What I mean by this can perhaps be illuminated by the following five categories.

The first is, undoubtedly, prior to his function as artist. He is an *enabling person*. Borrowing from systems analysis and dependent on Peter Rudge's book, *Ministry and Management*, I would say that the priest is responsible for implementing the learning community of the parish so that it is open to life, it is aware of its goals, and it makes the necessary internal adjustments to keep the one from obstructing the other. No artist functions in a vacuum, and the priest is responsible for developing the system in which he and others can fulfill their distinct role.

Second, he is a *resource person*. As any student of adult education can tell us, the learning agenda for people of the age upon which we are focusing in the parish community (eighteen to twenty-six, say) is established by them. We do not tell them what they ought to know but rather we respond to their expressed need to know. The tradition, the memory of the community, is not the sole possession of the parish priest, but he is the principal resource. He is part of the various structures that make up the learning community, he is skilled in listening, he knows how to reflect theologically, and he has a grasp of the past out of which the Christian community does its theology.

Beyond this, he is himself a *transparent person*. This is to say, in the third place, that he is undergoing personally the maturing process of which we are speaking here and can share it. He understands himself and his family well enough so that without bitterness or romantic fantasy, he can open his life to others. He can do this in his preaching (I believe that preaching is primarily witness), teaching, and in his personal pastoral contacts. It requires great sensitivity in order not to impose upon his family nor impose his family upon others. For example, my oldest daughter is at this point not the most enthusiastic church-goer, and I have told this to two worried married couples in the hopes that it might give them some support in a dilemma they were having with their children of the same age. Because, while I may be wrong, I do not sense any repudiation of the Christian faith and tradition here, but a simple disillusionment with its local embodiments (and maybe a need to try out new behavior). One person I told this to found assurance, another now frequently criticizes my method of child-rearing and does not feel at all supported by me.

As I list these categories, the intention is to move from the priest's role as a function of the learning community to the priest's role as a unique member of the community. The transparent person is a bridge (e.g., less a functionary of the group and more an individual among individuals). The fourth aspect, the *sacramental person,* seeks to define the integrity of the priest's person itself. Thomas Francoeur, a Roman Catholic educator, speaks of the priest as "manna person," and goes on to describe the presence of the priest within the families of his parish as one who bears within himself the presence of Christ. The children particularly come to know him as they would have known Christ, as friend and confidant. The relationship grows to where it follows naturally that they think of him as father of the community and as one to whom they go in their troubles (that is, as confessor and counselor).

The concept is profoundly gratifying, and yet it seems to me it is one very hard to conceptualize in pastoral theology. Perhaps it is easier to see that a pastor must sometimes be a surrogate father when the social father is absent, and this we can imagine readily on the basis of psychological constructs. But I am speaking of establishing a unique relationship with an intact family, beginning with the pre-marital conferences. The clergyman embodies as "God's artist" a transcendent witness who in subtle ways should be present in the first home of the newly married couple, during the pregnancy of the wife, at the birth of the child, and in that crucial first year or so of life. It is just at this time that many priests are noticeable by their absence. On the contrary, parish calling needs to concentrate here, and not on older, more established parishioners with whom we might feel more comfortable or from whom we might think we have more to gain.

Furthermore, it should be said that our society creates an aura about pregnancy, birth, and young parenthood that takes it as a time of unqualified bliss. This is simply not true. There are many intense negative feelings in the whole experience in even "normal" parents, and because of the taboo on such emotions they often feel very guilty and frustrated. A sensitive ministry of the sacramental person, involving the understanding and forgiveness of God, is as appropriate here as anywhere else.

Finally, the priest is the *ritual person,* he who presides at the Eucharist and proclaims the Word. It is to the sacred meal at which he presides that the young child comes with his parents, and therefore he is responsible for the form in which the child experiences the great symbol of the Eucharist. Because of its importance I want to comment on this experience in a section by itself; but first, perhaps, its importance needs to be emphasized.

A friend of mine—let's call him "Joe"—told me that as a seminarian he had occasion to take the eight-year-old adopted son of a mutual friend of ours to the Eucharist. The boy was not brought up in any Christian community, and being an inquisitive child, he asked all through the service what this meant and why they did that. After going to the communion rail with my friend, he asked him what the "pill" was that the priest gave, and Joe explained that it was "Jesus' body." "Oh, I see now," he said, "why it must taste bad! Everyone has such an ugly face after taking it!"

The Form of the Child's Experience of the Church

The child's experience of his parish church ought to be the same as that of his family. It needs to reinforce his openness to an end beyond himself, and to do it in a way that welcomes his imaginative participation and does not play upon the dark fears that are a part of every four- to six-year-old's inner life. Every priest knows the experience of being called "God" by a little child. Intellectual denials are beside the point; the child is building his understanding of his role and his acceptance in the whole cosmic order. If we keep this in mind and reflect on the nature of his encounters with God (or "God") at the parish Eucharist and the

Sunday School, something of the importance of the tone of his experience becomes clear.

It seems to me the important thing is that the child from the time of his baptism, when he is welcomed into the Christian community, needs to feel an acknowledgement of himself as a person known and loved *by name*. I am unhesitantly opposed to private, family baptisms. I am equally against "assembly-line baptisms" before crowds of hundreds of people, where no one can see the baby and no one hears his name, and where all is forgotten by the time we get to the offertory. Here again there is value in Christian communities of fifty or sixty—maybe neighborhood communities, as several have suggested to me—where a child is intimately known and grows up as a Christian.

Perhaps some would say that this need can be served by the Godparents, and yet Godparents present us with problems as well as opportunities. We are not too sure of their history. Apparently they go back to the witnesses in the early Church that vouched for the good character of the baptismal candidate. Today they serve more a social function—a way of honoring our aunts, uncles, brothers, and sisters—than a pastoral one. In a mobile society such as ours, it is rare that we live in the same community as our Godparents or Godchildren. So while sponsors can on occasion serve as a focus of the local congregation's responsibility to the child, it is probably unrealistic to think that three people can provide the sense of membership in the Christian community that we hope for.

For several years I have served a small congregation of approximately eighty baptized members under not altogether ideal circumstances. Yet upon reflection it seems to me that as young children are baptized, come to the nursery, join us for the Eucharist, and eventually come to make their communion, in this congregation they at least have the sense of being known. It is my custom to give the children small gifts—a cross or pendant of some kind—at the time of their first communion as a remembrance of that day. It is fascinating to see the way this takes on symbolic value for the child, and how he or she treasures and wears it to service. I do not think it is too farfetched to suggest that there is in the child's mind an equation between this gift and his feeling of acceptance among the members of the congregation.

I am not pleading for a limiting of the community experience to this smaller group (what I call in *The Future Shape of Ministry* the "sect"). There are dimensions of the religious life missing (the pageantry, the great music, the awe to be found in large space, the excitement of a crowd, etc.), which provide a different kind of emotional stimulation. There is a definite place in all our lives for this, but the value here lies in an intimacy, a joy found only in small groups and a freedom to be yourself when you are among people who know you. (It is in the context of such groups that the use of children's liturgies, as outlined in a book by that name published by the Liturgical Conference (Roman Catholic), finds a very important place.) As one person has suggested to me, a child making his communion among those who know him well is not so afraid of making a mistake or of having an accident. He knows that despite what may happen it is all right. As Parks Wilson, a Presbyterian minister who was of great help to me as a very young priest, once told me, this knowledge is the beginning of a real trust in God.

The Supportive Role of the Parish

The parish does not, as I hope is evident by now, prepare children for first communion. The parents do and will. Church school is not the place to prepare children and certainly any effort to create the mini-confirmation class is an avoidance of our real responsibility. I do not think that it is even up to the parish to decide whether or not unconfirmed children in their congregation are going to make their communion. People travel, and once a child has started in one parish, it would be pastorally disastrous to make him wait in another until he is confirmed. For this reason, I do not think that even dioceses and their bishops can long pretend that they have an option. Pandora's box is open! Just as our children feel that what their friends can do they can do, so will families believe that what one parish and diocese can do so can the other.

The immediate parochial task—having outlined the long-range parochial task—is twofold: the preparation of the parents (including the recommendation and provision of material), and the appropriate celebration of the first communion.

In preparing parents we begin by reminding them from time to time that the responsibility for deciding when a child shall make his first communion rests between them and their child. This can be done in bulletins, newsletters, chancel announcements, parish brochures, special letters, etc. It can also be a subject when making parish calls. With the information should come the priest's interest in meeting with parents who, with their children, have arrived at an affirmative decision. The purpose for this conference is to determine how the parents might receive preparation, to minister to any anxieties or to answer any questions they might have, and to set the date of the first communion. The date is important, because whether or not it be an occasion of a big celebration, it is a time which should not pass without congregational notice. This should be a great event for the child and it would be insensitive to ignore it within the parish family.

The kind of formal, group parental preparation provided by a parish depends on the parish and the material provided. I shall list here some of the curricula that are available, and in so doing shall indicate the parental training expected. It is, however, one of the structures to which I have referred earlier in this chapter that provide the Church with a way of focusing its ministry in a crucial area. It is a form of adult Christian education, and therefore is of wider value than just the immediate issue. By all means, let us capitalize on it. I would hope that beyond a discussion of the material to be used, there would be a thorough examination of the whole rationale of what the Episcopal Church is now doing, with a close reading and discussion of this book and perhaps some related resources.

Obviously the preparation of the parents is not done without some idea of how the parish intends to celebrate the first communion of its children. This is the projected act to which the discussion groups, the material, and the parental sessions with their children are the means. Therefore, the advance notices and the sessions with the parents must be shaped with this in mind.

It might be that the parish intends for this occasion to be more or less *ad hoc,* depending on when the parents think appropriate. Therefore, individual children will be making their first communion on any given Sunday at any scheduled Eucharist. Certainly this will happen occasionally without planning of any kind, when a child unknown to the priest offers himself spontaneously for communion. It would be wrong to deny him.

It is also another option that if a Church School class is to make its communion as a group, a special Eucharist, perhaps in the classroom, might be celebrated by the priest and the children. This same extracurricular type service might be related to a neighborhood gathering, such as Westerhoff proposes for the education of Christian families. If there are within the parish various "sects," it would be altogether appropriate that the first communion of a member be at a Eucharist offered in a home or at the parish church in the company of that group. The possibilities here are quite extensive.

A third alternative would be a special Eucharistic festival, which would be the annual or semiannual celebration of new communicants. Perhaps if the children had already made their first communion on their own, this Sunday we would still direct the parish's attention to the new status of the children and share with them their joy at such an event. It would be an occasion for letting the imagination of all play upon the possibilities for participation of all in terms of processions, music, banners, art, lights, reading, preaching, and so forth. You might say that it would be a Feast of Corpus Christi in terms of a contemporary rather than a medieval consciousness.

As a way of reporting what has been done elsewhere in building this program, from having the parents notice the new order of things to the actual celebration of the first communion, I would include here excerpts of letters from two parish priests to their people which

I think are very helpful. The first is from the Rev. Noland Pipes, curate of St. James' Church, Alexandria, La.

Dear Friends:

As the parent of two children who are baptized but unconfirmed, I think I know some of the questions that come to mind when we start talking about the admission of children to Communion prior to Confirmation. Here are three that come to my mind.

> If our children are to be receiving Communion before Confirmation, what then is the purpose of Confirmation and how will they receive the instruction we have usually required?

> What kind of preparation will be available to these younger children so that they may be ready to receive Communion?

> Who will decide when a particular child is ready, and will parents be given help in explaining the meaning of Communion to their children?

We plan to deal with these and the other questions which you may have at the special meeting called for this Tuesday night. There will be other meetings offered by your parish clergy, but this one is crucial . . . .

At the time this letter was sent out, the Diocese of Louisiana had not decided when to initiate this practice and so there was no definite date to which they were looking. But Fr. Pipes drew his parishioners into an involvement in the issues centering in this new practice.

A second example of pastoral support is from the Chapel of the Cross, Chapel Hill, N.C., where the rector, the Rev. Peter Lee has a specific program set up, with a date for the celebration of first communions.

Dear Friends:

This letter is especially important for parents of children who are not confirmed, but I ask every member of the parish to read through it. . . .

Our church, over a long period, has been led to a position common among many Christian communions the world over: baptism is the rite of initiation into the Christian family and that Holy Communion is the rite of nourishment in the family. No baptized person, therefore, should be denied the Sacrament, whatever his age.

The new rule, opening the Sacament to all baptized children, indicates a refreshing humility in the church's approach to the Sacrament. Under the former rule, the church assumed that confirmation instruction provided young people an understanding of the Sacrament necessary before receiving it. Now, the church admits that few adults have any comprehensive intellectual grasp of the mystery of the Holy Communion, and, as very young children can understand the affection behind their parents' care, so they can comprehend in some measure spiritual feeding at the Lord's Table. The Episcopal Church throughout the country is moving to the position that a Christian should not be able to remember a time when he was *not* fed at the Lord's Table. . . .

On Sunday, May 23, 1971, we will have a parish communion festival at which all baptized persons will be welcome at the Lord's Table. In practical terms, since our custom is for nursery and kindergarten children to go directly to their classrooms, the service will involve children in the first grade and above.

The church's rule, however, is clear. No baptized person—

however young—will be denied the Sacrament if he comes to the Altar. In initiating the new rule in the Diocese of North Carolina, the Bishop and the Diocesan Liturgical Commission suggest some weeks of preparation . . . and suggest that children should be able to walk to the altar! That is an indication of the church's serious intention that a Christian sacramental life should begin very early.

What about your child? First, he should want to come to the Sacrament and should not be forced . . . . Children, when they are prepared and when they so desire, should go to the altar with their parents. Their concern should not be how to receive Communion correctly but rather interest and curiosity in sharing with their parents this central act of Christian fellowship.

With very young children, a parent may want to receive the wafer, break it in half, dip it in the chalice, and give it to his child. When a child can imitate his parent, he can receive the wafer himself and take a sip from the chalice himself. It may be wise for small children to stand rather than to kneel. Parents should not hesitate to speak quietly to their children at the altar rail, giving them gentle instructions on the spot. . . .

I invite parents and all adults to join . . . in helping young people appreciate the centrality and richness of the Holy Communion. The service on May 23rd will be a festival of our parish family, and should mark another occasion when we demonstrate to the community our unity in the Christ who feeds us at his table.

This is a much longer letter, which seeks to provide information and support that perhaps could be given in a parent's discussion group. But at the same time it is very pastorally sensitive, and has the great virtue of drawing the whole parish—including those without small children—into the meaning and celebration of the event! I suspect that the reader will find, as I do, Fr. Lee's suggestions as to the "logistics" of a small child's communion very helpful, even though parish custom varies; for example, as regards even adults kneeling for communion or feelings about intinction.

One further example on the level of diocesan rather than parish programming might be noted here. The Diocese of Connecticut has developed some materials to guide the local parish in supporting the communion of their children, together with a statement from its bishop. Interestingly enough, admission to communion is to be authorized by the bishop, who will grant a certificate acknowledging this. I assume that this policy is intended to underline the importance of this event for the child (which is fine, if it does) and perhaps to assure the hierarchy of its control over the procedure. It seems to me questionable, however, as to whether this emphasis on bigness will mean that much to the child. Furthermore, I am made uncomfortable by the apparent need to "check this out with headquarters." What we need is more trust. This goes as well for the guidelines, which tend to emphasize "instruction" centered in the parish, rather than "formation" in the home. In my opinion this is not going to get the job done.

A Listing of Resources

JoAnn Marie Angers, *My Beginning Mass Book* (Twenty-Third Publications), $1.25. Pictures and coloring activities to introduce first to third graders to involvement in the Eucharist.

Richard Chilson, *Living in the Lord: Easter Sacraments for Young People* (Doubleday/Nazareth), $3.50.

Discusses baptism, confirmation, and the Eucharist in simple terms.

Iris V. Cully, *We Give Thanks* (Morehouse-Barlow), $1.95; Teacher's edition, $4.50; Guidebook for Parents, $1.95. Ten sessions of preparation for receiving Holy Communion, including a workbook for use at home. Familiarizes children with worship.

Urban T. Holmes, *Praying with the Family of God* (Winston), $7.50; Leader's Guide, $3.95. Ten 1-hour sessions explaining the Book of Common Prayer to children.

John Kater, *Another Letter of John to James* (Seabury), $4.95. An explanation of the Eucharist in words and pictures, suitable for young children.

Joanne Lopez Kepes, *God's Wonderful World and Me* (Peter Li), $7.95. Suitable for preschoolers.

Geiko Muller-Fahrenholz, editor, . . . *And Do Not Hinder Them: An Ecumenical Plea for the Admission of Chidren to the Eucharist* (World Council of Churches), $3.95. A collection of essays by theologians of various traditions in favor of an early age for admission to the Eucharist.

Together at the Lord's Supper (Winston), $3.25; Leader's Guide, $4.95; Parent's Book, $2.25. First communion preparation for fifth and sixth graders in six lessons. This program was developed in consultation with Lutheran educators.

It's All About Eucharist (Winston), $5.70; Leader's Manual, $1.75. Communion preparation for primary children in six sessions.

It's All About Celebrating (Winston) consists of a set of student leaflets ($7.50) and a leader's manual ($1.75) for use in families.

St. David's Press (The Episcopal Parish of St. David,

13000 St. David Road, Minnetonka, Minn. 55343) prints
two sets of letters, both aimed at first to third grade
readers. No. 1 is a set of communion letters ending with
an invitation to first communion. No. 2 is a set of
communion enrichment letters, pretty much the same
material but aimed at children who have been communicating for some time. Each set costs $1.75
complete.

Some Problems

Perhaps it is bad "psychology" to conclude with a
few problems for which I claim no final answers. But a
new practice will raise issues that perhaps we never
thought about, and it might be helpful if at least an
awareness is expressed, as well as the hope that together we might work out some of the rough spots.

For a long time now the Episcopal Church has kept
count of herself in terms of baptized persons, communi-
cants-in-good-standing, and confirmed persons not in
good standing. By canon law (Title I, Canon 16, Sec. 3)
a communicant-in-good-standing is a confirmed person
who has received communion at least three times in the
calendar year. In admitting children to communion, the
House of Bishops stipulated that they shall *not* be considered "communicants." This seems to me a kind of
double-talk of which we will continue to be guilty until
we pursue our actions to their logical conclusion. A person who makes his communion is a "communicant."
What we need is canonical revision which counts Christians by baptized membership, adding perhaps "in-
good-standing," and forgetting the fine distinction involving confirmation.

I have also had it suggested to me that once a child

makes his first communion he should not be encouraged to repeat the action too frequently. This I do not understand. It would seem only right to me that Sunday School schedules be arranged so that regular weekly communion is possible. There is a problem in parochial schools where there are many non-Episcopal children, and even some non-Christian ones, and it is the practice for all students to attend the Eucharist as a group once or more a week. If some children make their communion and others do not on such occasions, there will be a tendency to polarize the classes. For myself this raises the question of why we have the Eucharist at all where non-Christian children are required to attend. It would seem to me better to have such attendance optional than the alternative of non-communicating Eucharist (which obviously would be a denial of everything I have written in this book).

Another question that is raised for which I am much less ready with an answer involves the baptized but non-confirmed adult who presents himself to the priest asking what steps are necessary for him to make his communion and consider himself a member of this parish and the Episcopal Church. It may seem obvious to some that this has not changed. He takes instruction and gets confirmed. But what is confirmation? We did not accept letters of transfer from other Christian bodies, as I recall, because (explicitly or implicitly) we did not believe their initiation "complete." We now operate in terms of a theology which makes this nonsense. It seems to me that this whole practice is undercut and we must work out some new ways of handling this. Routine conditional rebaptism, as formerly practiced in the Roman Catholic Church, will not do.

Finally, with a heavy thrust toward family involvement, what happens to those without family connections or, at least, without present children or grandchildren? The answers here are not easy, but an awareness is necessary. My call here has been to a certain focus of ministry, because it seems to me that the human sciences tell us that herein lies the heart of religious training. But I do not intend for us to neglect other points in the life cycle. If such people are left out of the learning community, then we have somehow failed in all we have sought to do. The task before us is to make a beginning in infusing the entire lived experience of man with the love of Christ.

Appendix:
Audio-Visual Resources

One form of support which the parish community can lend the family is the use of certain audio-visual materials in the course of the young child's life within the church program. Just how this can be coordinated with the admission of children to communion depends largely on how that matter is handled in the parish. Obviously an individualized approach will suffer the handicap of not directly relating this material to what is going on in the home instruction. This could be overcome in those parishes which can afford to own and provide the equipment and filmstrips for home use. In other situations, however, we will have to be satisfied with a less immediate relationship of all the factors involved. In parishes where we build toward one or two occasions in the year when groups of children are admitted to communion there can be closer coordination on the congregational level.

The audio-visual material available is not of the quality and quantity that seems at first to exist. Apparently it is not easy to develop materials for the primary age of this kind, and what is advertised is often more appropriate for an older age. In reviewing materials, I have based my judgments on an age group from five to seven.

Materials available from the Thomas S. Klise Co., Box 3418, Peoria, Ill. 61614: *The Man for Others* (four filmstrips, two cassettes on the message and mission of Jesus) and *This Sunday Party* (two filmstrips and two cassettes for first communion), costing $50.00 and $40.00 respectively. These materials are colorful, up to date in their theology,.and technically well produced. In fact, they are so professional that they appear almost slick in their earthiness. The art work may appeal to some; I personally find it a little too "artsy craftsy." My principal objection is that the narration throws out a great many ideas, some of them utterly beyond the comprehension of those for whom it is intended. In previewing it in class and with groups of clergy I find a general consensus that it appeals probably much more to the adult who finds it very supportive of post-Vatican II insights, than to children, whom it seems to miss completely. Perhaps parts of *This Sunday Party* could be used with profit.

Materials available from Winston Press, 430 Oak Grove, Minneapolis, MN 55403; *Our Church for The Episcopal Child* (Series A,B,C), $4.25 each; Teacher Guide (all 3 series), $1.50. For use separately or with *Our Episcopal Church Filmstrips,* $79.95 (complete with cassettes). For primary children. Two of the four filmstrips deal particularly with the Eucharist. *Our Church for the Lutheran Child* (Sets A,B,C), $3.85 each; Teacher Guide (all three sets), $1.95. For use separately or with *Our Lutheran Church `Filmstrips,* $59.95 (records or cassettes). Introduction to worship includes preparation for Holy Communion. *A Praising People,* $29.95 (filmstrips with records or cassettes). Includes comprehensive

Leader Guides. *Churches* explores ways the worshiping community has expressed its identity in church architecture and furnishings. *The Eucharistic Prayer* looks at the form and spirit of the Holy Communion service and its roots in Jewish tradition.

Materials available from ROA, 6633 W. Howard St., Niles, Ill. 60648: the newer filmstrips available from ROA that would be useful with small children are: *To Be a Christian Child* ($175.00), *Children of Light* ($215.00), *The Secret* ($215.00), and *Little People's Scripture Stories* ($325.00).